30

42

9933

INTELLIGENCE
on Myths and Measurement

ADVANCES
IN
PSYCHOLOGY

3

Editors

G. E. STELMACH

P. A. VROON

NORTH-HOLLAND PUBLISHING COMPANY
AMSTERDAM · NEW YORK · OXFORD

INTELLIGENCE
on Myths and Measurement

Pieter A. VROON

Psychological Institute
University of Leiden
The Netherlands

1980

NORTH-HOLLAND PUBLISHING COMPANY
AMSTERDAM • NEW YORK • OXFORD

ISBN: 0 444 85465 7

Publishers:
NORTH-HOLLAND PUBLISHING COMPANY
AMSTERDAM • NEW YORK • OXFORD

Sole distributors for the U.S.A. and Canada:
ELSEVIER NORTH-HOLLAND, INC.
52 VANDERBILT AVENUE
NEW YORK, N.Y. 10017

Library of Congress Cataloging in Publication Data

Vroon, P   A
    Intelligence.

    (Advances in psychology ; v. 3)
    Bibliography: p.
    1. Intellect. 2. Intelligence tests. I. Title.
II. Series: Advances in psychology (Amsterdam) ; 3.
[DNLM: 1. Intelligence. 2. Intelligence tests.
W1 AD798L v. 3 / BF431 V984i]
BF431.V7613   153.9   80-10853
ISBN 0-444-85465-7

There are four chief obstacles to grasping truth, which hinder every man, however learned, and scarcely allow anyone to win a clear title to knowledge; namely, submission to faulty and unworthy authority, influence of custom, popular prejudice, and concealment of our own ignorance accompanied by the ostentatious display of our knowledge.

Roger Bacon

TO THE READER

Psychology is about people. That is one of the few things we agree upon. People have opinions about themselves and others. Someone is stupid, assertive, or has an inferiority complex. A part of this usage points to phenomena that have been examined empirically for a century. The product of this consists of a growing stream of new terms and explanations that are often being included in vocabulary. Because people do not understand themselves well it is not unthinkable that psychological jargon, intended as descriptive, leads to behaviour change.

Of all the qualities that people ascribe to themselves it appears that intelligence is still the center of attention. This applies to the individual, education, and the social order. Everyone is, directly or indirectly, familiar with IQ tests and with decisions that persons and groups come into contact with in this context. The enormous value that our culture affixes to intellectual faculties, especially in the verbal and numerical domain, has led to the fact that the research of this has not been restricted to a whisper in the laboratories. Moreover, everyone feels that they have something sensible to say about it. The result is that an awe-inspiring number of publications have been written. The various viewpoints about the origin of intelligence differences are known, with all their educational and political implications, as the turbid IQ debate. We already find initial phases of this in the history of philosophy but the problem became considerably sharpened when psychologists thought that they had discovered how to also measure intelligence. Thus, it appeared that the concept in question was considerably clarified and the drawn conclusions rose way above the level of vague speculating.

The inevitable result was that within psychology a vigorous quarrel between various theories arose. In general that is hardly interesting unless the quarrels have implications for society. With intelligence this is explicitly the case. One need only think of contradictory recommendations

concerning education. The issue has again arisen insofar that new trends
in other sciences, such as the so-called sociobiology, make far-reaching
pronouncements about psychological and social problems. This is not entirely new because a number of lines of reasoning and observations are already
4000 years old but were rediscovered. Again the question centers on the
extent to which numerous behaviours rest on innate qualities and instincts
where little can be changed. According to various sociobiologists, man
must adapt himself to his nature and that means that all types of objectives
of the social sciences can be ordered under the unattainable utopias. If
this variant of biology is correct it means bankruptcy for a large selection
of the social sciences.

Sufficient reason therefore to line up a number of issues from the
past and the present. Obviously this has been done before. Intelligence is
an elusive concept that lends itself to numerous contemplations and non-
committal speculations. It is not the intention of this book to supply yet
another opinion and interpretation. Rather an attempt is made to find out
how to get a grip on this concept on a scientific level. In the literature
concerning this the strange phenomenon occurs that the enthusiasm, alias
the preconceived opinions, of authors has often led to the literature being
chosen and described rather selectively. Many begin with their presuppositions and search for evidence that can always be found somewhere.
Although it is difficult to claim objectivity, in any case an attempt is
made in a detached manner to collect relevant material, unravel problems,
and draw conclusions. The last can be summarized as follows: reasoning from
an acceptable definition level, we virtually do not know what intelligence
is, and the nature-nurture controversy is meaningless for the time being,
no more than it is useful to establish in which corner of a dark room a
black cat is sitting when we do not even know if it actually exists.

Here we confront a dilemma that at present we can write about human
qualities, and therefore also about intelligence, in at least two ways.
There is a, to some extent, literary angle that facilitates reading for
many. The problem is then, however, that the explanation of the way in
which a test is made, what scores mean, and the question what the various
viewpoints actually contain, must be omitted with the result that the
reader is mainly informed in terms of vagueness. Besides this there is a
quantitative-statistical angle that is of great importance to be able to
judge research, but through which the tendency of the problem in a broader
context can easily be lost. Hence, an attempt to unite both aspects. This

means that statistical and methodological questions that cannot be avoided are interwoven in the various topics in the chapters.

Thanks are extended to Dr. J. de Leeuw who never ceased to supply material and who conscientiously read the manuscript, and to other colleagues who, whether or not in the form of conversations, provided necessary stimulation. The text was translated by Angie Pleit-Kuiper. The responsibility for this book remains with the author.

Leiden, July 1979

CONTENTS

1 INTELLIGENCE: HISTORY OF THE CONCEPT

It is not true that the meaning of a word becomes clearer according to how often we use it. How many know exactly what a volt is, apart from the fact that bodily contact with many could prove hazardous? Concerning terms that are related to human behaviour it is even more apparent that language has both a naming and a concealing property. Words such as I, self and consciousness are used continuously; courses even exist to learn about these concepts, but the question asking exactly what is meant here, as a rule remains unanswered.

A term that also plays an important role is intelligence. Daily usage rarely provides a clear definition. Intelligence appears to have something to do with cleverness, the ability to obtain a highschool diploma, the competence to cope as an independent grocer in the midst of supermarkets, and the possession of tax evasion techniques. In short, intellect is brought into context with visions of getting ahead in society. Perhaps this might be the reason why politicians make statements related to this, some of which are supported by psychologists, who take an interest in the social order[1]. From concerned declarations in political speeches it is heard that society is more complicated, more pluralistic and more problematic than ever. If we wish to cope in the future, educating problem-solvers is of utmost importance. The most difficult problems and the greatest influence must be put in the hands of the most capable. Intellectualism and meritocracy are almost unavoidable. However, capability is scarce. Only a small percentage of the population can attain a doctorate, almost no one can become a chess master, pianist or great orator. Everybody has his own limits and for most people these are all too swiftly attained. Time and effort can do little to change this situation. Selection by intelligence, therefore, becomes a necessity.

According to some philosophers, history is eternal repetition. They are partly right since we already find this viewpoint with Plato, who puts the rule of state in the hands of the keepers (ἀρχωντεσ), that is, specially

1

selected men who, after many decades of training are then given the strings
to pull. Other reason more along lines of the supposedly ironic first
passage of Descartes' main work, where the philosopher explains that common
sense is the best distributed gift in the world because everyone believes
to possess more than sufficient. Many complain of a bad memory; few,
however, of a poor intellect (this we prefer to attribute to others).
People are equal, or at least, alike. Everyone should be given the same
opportunities, and, if possible, the same remuneration. Selection is
necessary, but must occur with great caution. Psychology must guard against
being used as an instrument by those in power, as their interest basically
lies in maintaining existing inequality.

    In this way, two general ideas related to intelligence are outlined,
which do not go beyond the level of monumental vagueness. As science is
not an alien concern, we find these traditionally elitist and egalitarian
viewpoints returning, with all the nuances that lie between, in psychological
research concerned with the nature of our intellectual abilities and the
origin of the differences between persons. Especially the latter is important because, according to the conclusions drawn, rather far-reaching
recommendations are sometimes given regarding the educational system and
the social order in its generality. A look at philosophy is useful to be
able to express something about the history of the concept.

Philosophy

    The concept of intelligence is not a recent invention by psychologists.
The psychic abilities are traditionally split up into knowing, feeling, and
wanting, and this division has ancient roots. Reflections on the nature of
man belong to the philosophical domain, a discipline that can be summarized
as a specialism aimed at universal problems. Regarding the theory of
evolution, it can be questioned whether development should be conceived as
progress or merely as continuation. The same applies to philosophy, which
means that in considering the past there need not necessarily be a trend.
Moreover, it appears to be exceptionally difficult to devise propositions
which philosophers agree upon. Nevertheless, an attempt.

    The oldest sources available relating to western thinking are the
writings of Homer and Hesiod[2]. It is noteworthy that, according to some, in
these texts words do not, or rarely, appear which evidently have something
to do with devising and reasoning. Although there are various terms which

relate to the activity of organ⌐, references to the brain are lacking, a
situation which appeared to last up to and including Aristotle (he limited
the task of the brain to cooling down the heat of the heart). When Homer
and Hesiod can not finish their account, they call in external forces (e.g.
the muses) to tell them how to continue. It seems that these poets and
writers experienced themselves as entities which were rather dependent on
inspirations from elsewhere. Significance was attached to drinking and
breathing (being inspired) which are presently conceived of as an internal
process (thinking). Emotions were not described and appointed more or less
abstractly, but were linked to the changes which respiration and heartbeat
(θϋμοσ, κραδίη) underwent from moment to moment, or to sensations that
possibly occurred in the abdomen (ήτορ). Where cognitive processes are
mentioned, the νόοσ is discussed, presumably to be seen as a type of mind's
eye. In fright or in recognition of something or someone, the φρηνεσ play
an important role. This is usually interpreted as "spirit" or something
similar. There are, however, indications that the lungs are involved. For
people who rarely deal in abstractions, this word is not so badly chosen.
Respiration reflects the condition in which we find ourselves - we catch
our breath when frightened, we hold our breath at an unexpected event, and
so on. It was said of Socrates later that his *breast* was full of thoughts.
Some classicists feel that in those days people's psychic functioning
differed from ours; that thinking, knowing and recognizing were processes
that caught one and that, therefore, these were not felt to be personal
possessions. The concrete experiences, especially experiences linked to
bodily sensations, are summed up in the proposition that breath, in early
days, can be described as "the stuff of consciousness", that thoughts
coincide with words and words with breath. In summary: emotional and
intellectual functioning were mainly experienced in and ascribed to various
physiological processes throughout the entire body. The brain, however, was
unimportant because it did not produce differentiated sensations. There
are perhaps indications that something similar applied to the Jewish people.
In Ez. 3:4, at least, we read: "take care that your *beten* (abdomen) eats and
fill your *mo'im* (intestines) with this scroll; then go up to the house of
Israel and speak my words to them". It almost seems that the concept "person"
meant something different in those times. Expressions which directly relate
to thinking, reasoning, and use of judgment are abundantly found in the
younger books of the Old Testament.

   If the nature of thinking and experience can be judged by usage, there

were considerable changes made in Plato's time. His descriptions of mental
functioning are not only much more abstract, but he also makes a distinction
between two forms of knowledge with which we are still familiar. On the one
side he names the λόγοσ, which seems to have to do with the ability to
reason, and διάνοια on the other side, which presumably means something
along the lines of perceiving, contemplating, realizing, or recognizing.
With Aristotle, the concept νουσ (related to νοείν - to see) is an abstract
ability to think; νόησισ is the actual process of understanding. The Romans
translated λογοσ as *ratio* (our rational, reasonable), νουσ became *intelli-
gentia*. This division of reasoning opposed to realizing is long maintained
in the history of philosophy as *ratio* and *intellectus*. Augustine compares
the latter with contemplating and realizing[3]; and in the eighteenth century
Kant speaks about *Verstand* and *Vernunft*. Intellectually and sensorially
attained knowledge are usually placed against one another, which we also
find in profusion with Kant[4]. In general, many philosophers consider
intellect to be the most important human ability. Thomas Aquinas describes
God as a spiritual being in terms of "pure knowledge" (*intellectus purus*),
and also Spinoza considers reason to be the center of human actions[5], to
mention just a few examples.

The differentiation of psychic functions probably caused people to
start questioning their origin. Traditionally, rationalism and empiricism
oppose one another. According to Plato, the body belongs to material, mortal
and imperfect phenomena; the soul and reason, however, stem from the world
of the immaterial, immortal and perfect ideas. Plato also felt that
experience plays a subordinate role in the assimilation of knowledge. The
senses lead us to knowledge via the mechanisms of memory (ἀναμνησισ), that
is, knowledge lies dormant in man and the senses are only a sort of reminder
to the mind, allowing us to recall what we already know. In the seventeenth
century Descartes provided a variant for this with his suppositions concerning innate ideas. Trends in contemporary psychology which emphasize certain
forms of given knowledge, are called nativistic. Up to a point, we can use
the psychoanalyst Jung as an example, who believed that each individual is
in contact with a collective unconscious, that is, a great number of
experiences poured into models (archetypes) and visions that mankind has
acquired over millenia. The linguist Chomsky says that the use of language
has to do with competence or an ability that cannot be related back to
experience, to use of syntax (the whole of formal rules).

The rival of rationalism is empiricism, which reduces knowledge wholly

to experience. The philosophers of the Stoa are an old example. According
to them, man is born with a mind which can be compared to a papyrus scroll
which lies ready to be written upon. Sensations lead to images (φαντασια)
that can be understood through the mind (καταλήψισ) and then transform into
abstract concepts (έννοιαι). Strictly speaking, nothing is innate, but
certain concepts originate of themselves. These are general concepts
(κοιναι έννοιαι) referring to morality, the existence of God, and life after
death. In the seventeenth and eighteenth century empiricism arose, especially in England. The mind is, according to Locke, a *tabula rasa*, that gets
written by the senses. Berkeley gives a concise definition of empiricism:
"the mind has nothing that was not contained in the senses before." "Nothing,
except the mind itself," added the apparently dissatisfied Leibnitz[6],
thereby paving the road for Kant's theory of knowledge, which can be viewed
as a synthesis of rationalism and empiricism. A psychological translation
of empiricism is the behaviourism of Watson et al., who considered innate
factors to be of little importance.

Kant's theory of knowledge, which is especially set out in the *Kritik
der reinen Vernunft*, can be summarized as follows. Kant explains that all
knowledge begins with experience, but does not spring forth from this. He
aims at a mechanism which shows some resemblance to the philosophy of the
Stoa. Man is equipped with reason, which is associated with sensorial
information in three ways. Perceptions are placed in the *Anschauungsformen*
of space and time. Secondly, there is an arrangement in twelve logical
categories such as causality, and finally, knowledge is coordinated into
three general ideas, i.e. that the world, God, and the soul exist. In this
way Kant makes a distinction between thinking on the one hand and reality,
to which that thinking is related, on the other. Reality itself (*das Ding
an sich*) is imaginable but not knowable because we cannot step outside our
range of thinking. Thinking is an entity from which a certain structure is
forced upon the world. Kant's theory of knowledge includes, therefore, both
rationalistic and empirical elements. Experience is the key to the world,
but *the* reality is, as in Plato's thoughts, *blosz intelligibel,* or merely
to be imagined. Also, this idea appears more or less in psychology, namely
in modern cognitivism (Neisser et al.)[7].

To commence, we can say that rationalism and empiricism are related to
two trends that today still quarrel vehemently about the origin of
differences in intelligence: the nature and the nurture theory. Incidentally,
it must be mentioned that this dispute in philosophy does not take the

foreground very distinctly; a rational or empirical viewpoint was adapted
regarding man in general, where relatively little interest was shown for
individual differences. What can be defended is that these trends in the
past were related to politics. There are connections between empiricism
and egalitarianism, and between rationalism and elitism. Indications can be
found in various writings of philosophers such as Locke, Hume, Mill,
Voltaire and Rousseau.

Predestined Development

The division of minds within the philosophy of knowledge has affected
the ideas which traditionally existed about the nature of human development.
Long before the theory of evolution and genetics made their debut, it was
postulated that many human qualities were innate. In the Hammurabic Code
of approximately 1750 B.C., rules are set out in relation to this[8], and we
also find examples in the Bible (Lev. 18). Plato considered that an important part of behaviour was *not* learned, and Seneca in the *Quaestiones Natu-
rales*, conveys an all but genetic theory where he says that all the
qualities of man lie confined in the sperm. Words with an identical tendency
are handed down from Hippocrates.

The theory of predestined development has close connections with
theology[9]. During the Middle Ages the term state (from *status*, condition)
was not only utilized to indicate society, but the state of marriage was
also mentioned, the virginal state and the state of sin and mercy. Man, as
we find written later in the Heidelberg Catechism, was not empowered to do
any good and inclined to all evil. He could not determine his own fate and
was at the mercy of higher powers, for good and for evil. Society was
stratified, including a hierarchy of heavens and angels, and each served
the whole to the glory of God. Concerning this, some took an intermediate
position. Pope Gregorius the Great believed that all men were created equal
but that according to God's command some are naturally placed above others.
The diversity is attributed to sin, which God balances by ordering the world
in a certain way. This means that man must accept his fate and that resistance is evil.

The doctores of theology played an important role in maintaining this
order. They were in direct contact with God because theology was regarded
as the highest science. They guarded against any encroachment. The

colleagues described each other in terms of *quasi stellae fulgebunt* (they
shine like the stars) and kept their spirits alert by proposing difficult
problems to each other. Examples are the questions: how many angels can be
put on the head of a pin, where the correct answer was "infinite" because
the problem dealt with immaterial, dimensionless beings; and the problem
whether a two-headed monster should be baptized twice. Cornelius Jansen,
the Bishop of Ieper, became the creator of the notorious Jansenism. It's
essence was that man's body and soul was afflicted with total depravity,
he had no free will (also postulated by Luther), and was dependent upon
possible divine mercy which was independent of one's actions. Heaven was
available to only a few and life was confined to predestination. According
to the philosopher Leibnitz, reality was only chaotic and incomprehensible
in appearance. In fact, there exists a *harmonia praestabilita*, a predestined
harmony in which man could and should change nothing and which makes our
world the best of all worlds. Similar ideas appeared in biology and even in
psychology of a few decades ago[10].

So-called preformationism took a central position here. In connection
with pronouncements from Hippocrates and Seneca, Swammerdam noted that a
butterfly does not materialize out of nothing, but is already present,
folded up in its cocoon. On the basis of similar observations, Swammerdam
made a daring allegation where he says that the original sin is hereby
explained, because all persons were, after all, present in the organs of
Adam and Eve. In other words: we are a product of a past which fell into
sin and we do not possess the power to change ourselves. Other biological
researchers of that time demonstrated that perception and knowledge are
tightly interwoven and that we are inclined to see what we believe. Through
his primitive microscope, Hartsoeker thought he saw a complete human lying
folded up in the head of a sperm cell, and in the sperm of animals others
observed horses and donkeys. A problem that was readily spotted was how
monsters were created and, not lastly, the fact that in early stages,
embryos of various animals lookes exactly alike. Charles Darwin would later
explain that preformationism did not lie directly in the observable form,
but in determinants thereof, which were later named genes. Preformationism
means that much of behaviour is not learned, but is inherent to the organism.
In relation to this, the turn of the century brought the tropism theory of
Loeb, which purported that many behaviours (fototropism, heliotropism)
rested on stable connections with which living beings, from carp to man

were born. A little later followed the instinct theory of the psychologist
MacDougall and, not to be forgotten, the ethology of Lorenz and Tinbergen,
against which both heavy and neglected criticism has been given[11]. A movement which comes forth irresistibly in this context is the so-called
sociobiology[12]. Essential here is that many qualities and human possibilities,
from homosexuality, personality characteristics, intelligence to criminality,
are mainly determined by heredity. Wilson frequently uses one article to
prove this, while for each case many examples to the contrary exist.
Moreover, the observation of animals in their natural habitat would provide
invaluable information about our nature and about the desired social order.
A well-known example in which analogical reasoning is used with shattering
simplicity is Haanstra's scientifically supported Dutch movie "Like the
animals" (1972). A mammal urinates in regular distances in the steppes. This
means that he is defining his territory. The following scene shows an iron
garden fence, and there the evidence is provided. A large number of rats are
put in a cage. In time, the animals kill one another. Overpopulation, therefore, is undesirable which can be proven by the filming of a brutally
dispersed demonstration. No one will deny that ethological and sociobiological literature is interesting but that does not imply that there are no
dangers in this approach. One of these is that the sociobiologist purports
to come across "facts" in the animal world from which predictions can be
supposedly made about man. With the same right, however, we may fear that
the outlook to the scientific practitioner, without him realizing it, has
been influenced by human society, and that judgments and prejudices are
unnoticeably projected onto the animal world, after which these own products
are taken as facts. This is called the self-involvement of science, which
can play a nasty role, especially in the human sciences[13].

Within psychology, the same train of thought has been followed for a
long time and on a large scale. In the previous century, Stanley Hall set
his goal on becoming the Darwin of the human mind. The development of the
individual is a fast-motion film of the development of the species, an idea
that was connected to the biogenetic law of Häckel. This means that the
child's development, in short, manifests the history of thinking and
behaving of humanity and little can be changed in this process. Behaviour
is an unfolding of groups of innate reflexes. Development is maturation
which proceeds of itself, contended the well-known child psychologist Gesell,
and various types of upbringing and interventions are relatively meaningless. The same was defended by the Gestalt psychologists. Problem-solving,

for example, rests both in animals and man on an innate ability that
manifests itself in due course. Many publications of the child psychologist
and biologist Piaget relate approximately the same story. Cognitive, as
well as motor development, follows a relatively stable programming in time,
which is a complex way of stating that these matters are decided at birth
or, in any case, at a very early age[14]. In general, we can defend that the
theory of predestined development was dominant in (developmental) psychological literature up to and including World War II. Among other things,
this led to the fact that psychology largely consisted of measuring and
calculating correlations. Constructing theories about various processes,
including intelligence, was not considered to be of much importance.
Maturation did play the leading role and why should we burden ourselves
with the precise nature of processes about which nothing can be done anyway?
It is clear that this line of thought nourished behaviourism to the extent
that psychology became mainly the art of predicting behaviour. Regarding
content, a contradiction existed, however, to the extent that behaviourists
proposed an empiristical viewpoint and consequently, assumed that environment could completely shape the child. (Compare this to Watson's precept
about the dozen healthy infants.) This meant that in Europe, where
preformationism prevailed, the strivings of behaviourism (making predictions)
was partly taken over, but not the theory[15]. Concretely, this style of
thought meant that research about the alterability of behaviour, compensation programs, and so forth, was subject to little interest.

Equality and Liberalism

It is, however, incorrect to maintain that the thinking of all time
was wholly dominated by the theory of predestination and the fact that
people differ. Confucius is believed to have held the view that human
nature is the same for all and that differentiation of individuals only
rests on habit[16]. The reformation initially led to a more individualistic
attitude; personal responsibility was placed above institutions (the church),
functioning as a collective deliverer[17], and liberalism emerged. The classic
school in economics (Adam Smith) proclaimed the free market principle and
proposed that the government should minimally order, dictate, and intervene[18]. The best government was one that did the least. Still, this did not
mean that people were regarded as equal. In the book *Discours sur l'origine
de l'inégalité parmi les hommes*, published in 1754 by Rousseau, a distinction

was made between natural and moral inequality[19]. The first consists of
differences in health, bodily strength and intelligence; the second rests
on conventions and privileges and, therefore, must not carry the overtone.
In *Emile*, Rousseau does advocate equal educational chances, but natural
talents shall decide what the future will hold. We are still familiar with
this view from the expression "genius will emerge anyway", whereby we forget
to mention that we are only told this by geniuses who have actually emerged.
Also, in *Le contrat social* (1762) Rousseau states clearly: there are many
innate differences between people; equality should be that everyone receives
equal opportunity. Society should reward its individuals according to
services rendered (meritocracy), and not to descent. The slogan "all men
are created equal", was also equipped with a false bottom by Thomas
Jefferson in the *Preamble of the American Declaration of Independence*[20].
People are not born with the same capacities but have equal moral and
political rights and duties. Jefferson refers here to a natural aristocracy
consisting of individuals who, irrespective of their descent, possess great
innate talents. Society's task is not so much to offer everyone *equal*
opportunity, but *optimal* opportunity. In England, liberalism was defended
by the philosopher Herbert Spencer (1820-1903). Every governmental intervention was evil and one should leave things to take their natural course.
A background of liberalism was that society became multi-faceted and knew
countless professions. It was said that each individual should have
opportunity, but diversity must naturally be maintained, otherwise the
catastrophe would be immense. Moreover, such a complicated society has a
need for problem-solvers and they are scarce.

In this way, we are beginning to go round in circles and are ending
up again in the area of the predestination theory. Equal opportunity
- certainly - but people are not equal and they must not become so
considering the complexity of society. Biology, and later, genetics

Also in Germany, the constitution of Weimar (1919) stipulated that
society should give everyone the best opportunities. Talent required
stimulation, regardless of its social origin. However, both in Germany and
England it had already been apparent for a long time that the most
intelligent pupils in school came from the higher social classes. So, the
idea that talent was hereditary was apparent, according to some, although
Tawney (England, 1930's) pointed out that the educational level of children
had perhaps more connection to the bank accounts of their parents than to
their demonstrated intelligence.

supplied the justification for such political desires. Although Watson, the father of behaviourism, claimed in this century that all healthy individuals start out equal, many social scientists found biology and the predestination theory much more interesting and they pointed the behaviourists and their rats to the laboratory.

The Theory of Evolution

If there is one writing of the previous century that has been used and misused for many scientific and political purposes, then it is surely *The Origin of Species* by Charles Darwin (1859). Before, philosophers had placed man (predominately at least) in a spiritual world; now he is being compared with animals and he even appears to stem from them. Species appear, become confronted with changing circumstances, are able to adapt (via mutations) or not, and survive or become extinct. As the structure of industrialized society manifested, animals and man consisted of populations wherein characteristics followed distributions and cooperation was a necessity[21]. For psychology this meant that innocent forms of passing time such as the measurement of olfactory thresholds in order to test if some psychophysical law was valid, were supplemented with completely different activities. Prospective psychologists buried themselves in making the differences between people (differential psychology) measurable, in opposition to "mind in general" which was Wundt's view. Developmental theory was considered to be of great importance, and also social psychology, a branch of the tree of knowledge examining the contacts between people. Simultaneously, the comparative psychology of man and animal appeared.

A conflict arose within biology that partially contained social implications. In summary, Darwin claimed that populations with improper characteristics simply died out, while Lamarck postulated that acquired characteristics could become hereditary so that the specie could maintain itself. Lamarck lost the debate, also because of Mendel's work. For social reformers like the American sociologist Ward, who based his work on Lamarck, this constituted a catastrophe for the simple reason that a changing environment could neither take away from nor add anything to human nature[22]. Genes ignore the momentary environment, so that the quality of the race could only be influenced by manipulations based on the theory of heredity. Eugenics, or the theory of race improvement, was born. A second biological outlook on reality arose out of Lamarckian thinking and, until recently, was adhered to in the U.S.S.R.

In a medical respect, the previous century was dominated by a strange concoction of Darwin's and Lamarck's conceptions. Doctors felt that acquired characteristics were carried over to the next generation[23]. Conception was not limited to the joining of the egg and the sperm, but had something to do with the condensed reproduction of the attitude and life style of the parents. A woman who became insane had a great chance of bearing insane children, and with fatigue and drunkenness during coitus, the child became hereditarily burdened, as it was popularly called. Perceiving cow heads during pregnancy could result in a child with a face lik a cow. Postnatal jealousy and anger would poison the milk of the mother and lead to criminal children. Sexual hyperactivity was also harmful. In higher circles, wet nurses were often employed, but these were carefully selected since criminally-inclined women could carry their behaviour over on the child. In general, it was believed that the role of the father was basically over after coitus; the vicissitudes of the child were mainly dependent on the mother. In contemporary Persia, such nonsense led to the Shah repudiating the empress Soraya because she had not given him a son, while it was known that the sperm determines the gender.

Lysenkoism

Since 1917, the Soviet Union, is characterized, at a philosphical-ideological level, through dialectic materialism. This is not the place to have a discourse about that. In any case, one of the viewpoints is that man is not subject to his environment and that he can set himself on a higher plane in teamwork with material reality. In this respect, elated observations have been handed down from Trotski. "Man shall become unmeasurably stronger, wiser and more refined; his body shall become more harmonic, his movements more rhytmic, his voice more musical. The average man shall reach the heights of an Aristotle, a Goethe or a Marx. And above this level new geniuses shall originate." Within this framework, Lamarckian genetics fitted well. During the thirties the country was plagued with crop failure, so that the question arose whether new strains of plants could be cultivated quickly which would have better resistance against the elements[24]. Mendelian genetics did contribute solutions but these required more patience than one allowed oneself. The biologist Trofim Lysenko felt

that it was possibly to work at least four times faster, which promised an
attractive solution to a difficult problem. His train of thought was that
acquired characteristics became hereditary. This meant that seeds of plant
A, under deviant conditions, could become transformed into seeds of plant
B, or rather that changes in the environment leads, on short term, to
modification of hereditary characteristics. From 1935 to 1964 in the
magazine *Agrobiologiya*, many experiments were described from which it
appeared that without too much trouble, wheat could be transformed into
rye, barley into oats, firs into pines, and alders into birch. There was,
however, no mention of a test set-up that could withstand criticism.
Lysenko contended with these objections, supported by party officials, by
stating that these were expressions of "mathematical fetishism" and
"reactionary bourgeois science", this being totally in opposition to the
desired "proletarian" method of research. Serious opposition was suppressed
with the pronouncement that the involved members were sabotaging agricultural progress. The result was comparable to an operetta: books were written
by geneticists with Lysenko's views being defended, but they added Mendelian
appendices in jargon which censor officials could not understand. Lysenko
and his patron Kruschev simultaneously fell from power in 1964, after which
it appeared that the results were caused by mixing seeds and other forms of
carelessness, or, of you like, deceit.

Contemporary Russian psychology still shows traces of this that induce
some to praise it[25]. In relation to intelligence and school performance,
genetic arguments stand in the background. The development of psychic
functions is determined by society, the school, and not in the last place,
through the political system which claims to strive for maximal development
of all. It is not selection that is of interest and a necessity, but maximal
enrichment of everyone. Education must not accept given cognitive abilities,
but must create them; in this framework it is claimed that children can be
taught to think at a qualitatively higher level quite simply. Well-known
psychologists such as Luria and Vygotsky say that hereditary qualities do
determine the structure of the nervous system but that they hardly have
anything to do with the development of knowledge and skills. Within
dialectic materialism this statement is remarkable because the material
component of reality and man takes a central position. Behaviourism is
not highly regarded either. In the G.D.R. this trend is detracted as a
"mechanistisch verstanden Erfuhrungsgewinn", resulting in the slogan "die
Anlage potenziert, die Umwelt realisiert".

Besides, some general problems in reading Russian psychological literature are that the author often begins with an ode to Lenin, who was supposed to have foreseen, a half a century ago already, the reported experimental results, and that, as a rule, a very limited number of experimental subjects are used (often only one). The descriptions of research and procedures are often highly cryptic, and regarding the elaboration of the data, the simplest level of statistics is rarely passed[26]. However, there are indications that the tide is beginning to turn[27].

Classic Eugenics, Spencer and Galton

The pseudo-science of Lysenkoism implied that environmental variations quickly and predictably became expressed in the genes. The antipode of this viewpoint was eugenics. The work of Darwin and the connected subsequent publications of Mendel became widely read. A philosophical framework was provided by Herbert Spencer (1820-1903), and the American William Sumner (1840-1910), who can be classified as social Darwinists, that is, those who came to recommendations about the social order based on Darwin's theory[28]. Spencer felt that social differences can be explained genetically and that there is an inverse relation between the brain and the mechanism of reproduction. Both fight for the necessary nutrition and elements such as phosphorous. The poor are poor and dumb because they have an insufficiently developed nervous system. Their hereditary disposition makes sure that nutrition mainly follows a route to the genitalia, of which the result is that they form the most fertile group. The rich are rich and intelligent because their strong nervous system sucks the phosphorous upwards, causing lesser fertility and, consequently, less children. Crime, poverty, ill-health and infantile mortality are also caused by hereditary influences. The blacks in Africa became slaves because they were too stupid for something else and, in general, school results were naturally established by hereditarily determined intelligence. Sociologists such as Ward and Cooley protested in vain with the statement that perhaps the lower classes also contained many geniuses, but that due to shortcomings in the environment in which these children were raised, they missed their chances. It obviously makes a difference if the child must work on an assembly line fourteen hours a day, or is raised in a family where music is studied and the encyclopedia is memorized. However, their objections carried no weight.

If this continues, stated Spencer, the rapidly multiplying poor will cause man to become increasingly less intelligent, resulting in a mass descent to a subhuman level so that competition with the animals becomes necessary (again). Fortunately, rescue is available. The social order maintains that poverty will always exist and interventions by the government are completely unnecessary. The laws of nature make sure that there is a high rate of mortality among the poor through under-nourishment and many illnesses. Wars also lend a helping hand. The only measure that can be considered is sterilization of certain groups of the population. In Darwinism "the survival of the fittest" takes a central position. The poor were "unfit", according to Spencer, and would, therefore, be eliminated by natural selection. "If they are not sufficiently complete to live, they die and it is best they should die ... whoever is ushered into existence at the bottom of the scale can never rise to the top, because the weight of the universe is upon him." The goal of the social sciences, according to Spencer and Sumner, is not the exercising of social control but, on the contrary, to prove that such a control is impossible because of the laws of nature. It is obvious that both authors were very skeptical about democracy. Such form of government can mean that many persons who have no knowledge of anything could try to intervene, which only upsets the balance and causes a relapse. We also find Spencer's fear in the history of economics. Towards the end of the eighteenth century, Reverend Malthus had stated that if humanity continued along these lines it was doomed to destruction. According to him, the problem is that the number of people is growing along in geometrical progression and the means of existence (e.g. food) in arithmetical progression. Therefore, a shortage is in sight and will bring starvation and a high death rate.

Shortly after, Pearson was involved with the invention of the correlation coefficient. This is a number between -1 and +1 which indicates the strength and direction of the statistical relation between two or more variables, but which *never* says anything about the cause of the established relation. Pearson noticed that the correlation between parent and child in relation to the chance of contracting tuberculosis was .50, from which he concluded that this disease was genetically determined, and so it was not necessary to consider sanitation, health care and better nourishment. A personage worth mentioning from this time was also Professor Geel from Leiden[29]. He entitled the working class as "cursed common cattle who married before their eighteenth birthday, gorged on potatoes, bore consumptive children, collected welfare, and begged." The situation of the working class is illustrated by the fact that the children in Leiden, partly due to the long working days of their parents and to the lack of schooling, barely learned to speak. At the age of twenty they spoke a language that could barely be understood by "decent" citizens. Reading to them served no purpose because they could not understand the words and even the simplest poem or story was above their heads. Also noteworthy, was that in this time foreign workers were attracted to perform specialized jobs.

If social Darwinism pleaded for passivity from the government, eugenics went a step further. A very important man, in this regard, was Sir Francis Galton[30]. Galton (1822-1911) was a member of the English aristocracy, related to the Wedgwoods and to Charles Darwin. His father was a wealthy banker who presented Francis with a legacy large enough to allow him to leave the university at the beginning of his medical studies, so that he could spend the rest of his long life travelling, reading, and writing. Galton's scope of interest was very broad. He did much work in the area of meteorology, and published articles about cyclones, statistics, and biology. His publication list contains 227 items, including an article about prayer, written in 1872. Here he states that it was about time to find out whether prayer has any effect at all. According to him, this can be discovered by choosing two comparable groups from hospitals, one group of patients who pray, and another who do not, and to tally the number of deaths. Ministers make praying a profession, says Galton, but statistically it appears that they do not live longer than doctors and other aristocrats. It is to be feared, therefore, that prayer does not prolong life. The frequency of stillborn children is also the same in groups of various beliefs ("religious madness is very common indeed").

Subsequent test psychologists and admirers of Galton, such as the American Terman et al., assessed the IQ of about 300 deceased. Darwin had to work with a value between 135 and 140, Mozart had an IQ of 160, Goethe almost reached 190, and Galton became the record holder with a round 200. This value is based, among other things, on a letter of Galton's where he writes that at the age of four he was capable of reading every English book and, moreover, could recite 52 Latin verses.

The father of the famous Sir Cyril Burt was a doctor. As a child, Burt often accompanied his father and met Galton on one of these occasions. The description that Burt gives of Galton's appearance is moving. "He had a forehead like the dome of St. Paul's... However, he did not inherit what the family called the Socratic Darwin nose or the firm and slightly undershot

Darwin chin, both of them wellmarked Wedgwood characteristics." Galton's
skull was also inspected by phrenologists[31]. One of them came to the conclusion: "he has the largest organ of causality I have ever seen".

Galton was boundlessly interested in counting and measuring. "When-
ever you can, count" was his motto. He applied this, among other cases,
when his portrait was painted twice. The number of brush strokes appeared
to be about 20.000. He came into contact with the work of the Belgian
statistician A.J. Quetelet (1796-1874). In his book *Essai sur l'homme* he
described that measurements such as height and chest circumference fit into
a so-called normal, bell-curved distribution if they were taken from a
large amount of people[32]. In the case of the height of French soldiers,
Quetelet wrote that the average of the normal distribution reflected
l'homme moyen. Moreover, astronomers had observed that this same distribution gave an indication of measurement errors that one makes when observing
star transitions. It appears, therefore, that nature strives everywhere for
a certain average and that people deviate from the norm through coincidal
influences and disturbances. In view of the fact that many cases of this
variability were manifested and that height was considered to be hereditary,
Galton began to question whether the same distribution applied to other
(mental) factors, such as intelligence. Galton came to the realization that
with the help of Pascal's triangle, based on a finite number of measurements, the normal distribution could be reached (see chapter 3). Environmental variation was, according to Galton, substantial and unmeasurable.
Could not differences between people be more easily explained by assuming
that a finite number of genetic qualities are contained in the egg cell and
sperm?

Two other statistical concepts which played a large role in Galton's
theory are regression and correlation. Who exactly invented the correlation
coefficient is not clear but, in any case, one of Galton's publications from
1888 points to the fact that he also at least participated in this. According to Galton, the great importance of techniques such as the calculation
of regression and correlation, was that through the use of one bodily
characteristic many other characteristics could be described and predicted.
For example, it is possible to make statements, within a reasonable
boundary, about someone's height by measuring only the lenght of one leg.
The word correlation was chosen because of this connection between bodily
characteristics. Furthermore, regression and correlation offered the
possibility of speaking in terms of expectations about characteristics of

children on the basis of knowledge about the parents. If many characteristics are determined by heredity, which Galton felt was not only applicable to height, but also to intelligence, then it should be possible to make a forecast about the measured parents offspring. In this context, Galton utilized the so-called regression towards the mean of parent to child. This means, for example, that very tall parents have the tendency to bear shorter children. Until the seventies of this century, his followers describe this phenomenon as a mysterious force of nature that leads us to the average man. So far we have discussed some statistical instigations that have lead to Galton's theory of race improvement.

Within the framework of this ambitious project, Galton read widely and did much more work. He used the writings of Darwin as a base on a biological level, and he bridged the gap between biology on one side, and psychology and sociology on the other. He took over Darwin's ideas regarding natural variation, natural selection, and the heredity of physical characteristics, and projected these onto the mental plane, part of this being intelligence. Darwin had noticed that animals exhibited qualities that were a portrayal of the characteristics of its surroundings, and that these qualities came about through natural selection. Galton declared this assumption to be applicable to society. People too, are differently equipped, totally according to what society asks of them. Similar to the animal world, there are and must be differences to maintain the species. A society characterized by a division of labour demands individuals who show the capability to be versatile. The hierarchical structure of society is a result of innate differences. Social classes are not only a fact, but it is *good* that we have them since in this way the innate qualities are expressed adequately.

The moment had come to write the first book on this subject. It was called *Hereditary Genius, an Inquiry into its Laws and Consequences* and appeared in 1869. Galton writes: "I propose to show in this book that a man's natural abilities are derived by inheritance, under exactly the same limitations as are the form and physical features of the whole organic world." Next, he names the same points as Spencer: people differ and that is fine, but the ignorant poor multiply too quickly. Just as it applies to dogs and horses, it must, however, be possible through cross-breeding and birth control, to improve the human race and to set it on a higher plane. As a base for this Galton used, amongst other things, graphs which described brilliant families (such as Bach) and he analysed the origin of famous Greeks. It seems that Darwin almost immediately was very impressed with Galton's work. At least, in a letter dated December 23, 1869 he writes: "I do not think that I have ever in all my life read anything more interesting and original". Evolution no longer seemed an obtuse continuation, but it appeared that man had reached a point where he could intervene in the speed and nature of development. In this context, Galton explained his ideas further in three other books published respectively in 1874, 1883, and 1889.

This intervention must, of course, rest on something. Intelligence was (also) central in Galton's theory; the question was, therefore, how this entity could be determined so that the measurements could serve to take the necessary steps. Initially, Galton tried this by bringing "eminence" in relation to vicissitudes during the first years of life. He observed, for example, that various physicists in their youth had played with a type of Meccano box, but this provided a very slim base. Galton then proceeded to combine two ideas. The first one had a philosophical character, borrowed from Berkeley, among others, and implied that all knowledge comes to us via sensorial experience. The second was, as mentioned before, that mental qualities could be ascertained from bodily characteristics (a notion adhered to by Lombroso in criminology, the ideas about connected eyebrows, etc.), although earlier attempts in terms of brain weight, appeared to have no descriptive value. Thus, it was necessary to find an instrument that could serve as a starting point for race improvement.

In 1884 Galton founded the anthropometric laboratory in London. Height, weight, chest circumference, respiratory volume, muscle strength, and reaction time were measured from many thousands of people, and visual and auditory sharpnesses were determined. Particularly annoying was the outcome that many correlations with "eminence" reached no value of any significance. Strangely enough, this did not discourage Galton from his persistence in theorizing about race improvement. His recommendations are summarized as follows. If we wish to prevent man from becoming an animal again, a premium must be offered to intelligent persons who choose an intelligent partner. Galton considered it to be financially quite feasible to create a "galaxy of genius" in this way. The norm for the awarding of the premium was external characteristics and origin. The American psychologist J. McKeen Cattell (1860-1944) adopted this idea and promised each of his children one thousand dollars if they married the son or daughter of a professor. Furthermore, the government had to stipulate how many children one was allow-

ed to have, and for what price, by using an intelligence standard. This
system of premiums was named "positive eugenics". But the problems were not
all solved with this. The poor were still multiplying too quickly without
premium, so that a solution had to be found here also. This consisted of
"negative eugenics". In the book *Inquiries into Human Faculty and its
Development* of 1883, one can read on page 200 the catching phrase: "There
exists a sentiment, for the most part unreasonable, against the gradual
extinction of an inferior race".

Further information can be found in Galton's utopia *Kantsaywhere*
which, during his lifetime was not published for indistinct reasons (his
biographer, Pearson, did this later in the form of fragments). Ignorant
people must be placed under supervision, or better still, deported to
remote areas. Apart from this, a plea was made for seemingly progressive
measures such as the abolition of child labour. The reasoning behind this,
however, was that the poor families with many children would miss an
important source of income, which, on the one hand, would cause increasing
decimation, and on the other hand, would cause a halt in the inclination to
have more children. Furthermore, it was not the intention that everyone
would receive the right to vote, and the country would have to be governed
by a eugenic race, such as the previously mentioned "keepers" in Plato's
dialogue "The State".

Thus, historians suppose that Galton's advocated society had a fascist-
totalitarian character. It is remarkable that Galton, being an undefeatable
intellectual, drew a parallel between his theory and religion. The true
religion was the theory of evolution and the manner in which it could be
applied. Eugenics is actually a religion because the improvement of the
human race is the highest level to which we can aspire.

Eugenics Makes an Advance

It is definitely not true that these ideas were restricted to Victorian
England. Galton's influence in England lasted until after the second World
War, but the tragedy for Galton was that no government did anything which
concurred with his recommendations. However, elsewhere social Darwinism
and eugenics were adhered to strongly.

In America in 1904, the biologist C.B. Davenport persuaded the Carnegie
Foundation to finance a "Laboratory for Experimental Evolution", geared to
the improvement of the human race. The cross-breeding of humans was

investigated but was abandoned relatively swiftly because it was observed
with animals that annoying things could occur[33]. Many books appeared with
a strong racial tendency, such as Grant's *The Passing of the Great Race* and
Stoddard's work *The Rising Tide of Color against White Supremacy*. The
tendency was simple. The chaste American blood was threatened with thinning
by negroes and immigrants, and something had to be done about it. A quotation from Stoddard: "The old stock of American is today being literally
driven off the streets of New York City by the swarms of Polish Jews". Like
in Russia during Lysenko's time, geneticists did not protest, or hardly.
One reason could have been that they also relied partly on the Carnegie
Foundation for their research. Also psychologists contributed. Probably
the most familiar was Lewis Terman (1877-1956), who made an important
contribution to the development of intelligence tests. He stated that
genetic differences in intelligence between races and socioeconomic classes
do exist. IQ formed the basis of success in life; it was innate and, therefore, stable, with the result that a large portion of the psychology of
testing began to or should function as a sorting machine deciding which
people belonged in what profession and social class[34].

Other psychologists who offered themselves to the good cause were
Goddard, the inventor of the instinct theory William McDougall, and the
animal psychologist and statistician, Edward Lee Thorndike[35]. McDougall
noticed that diversity was necessary; we have no need for a group of
clumsy Einsteins. He made a plea to replace democracy with a caste system
based on biological appropriateness, including legal restrictions regarding
the amount wherein the lower classes were allowed to multiply and to
prevent marriages between members of different castes[36]. This is in
accordance with Davenport, who defended that intellect must simply be bred.
A breakthrough was reached in the period between the two world wars. Both
politicians and scientists expressed the fear that following the model of
the Russian Revolution, a revolt of the masses could occur. During World
War I, psychologists tested about 1.7 million recruits and advocated, on
the basis of the test results, to found a caste system and to introduce
measures to restrict immigration and even to promote sterilization laws[37].
One of these instigations was again originated by Terman. He had calculated
that 1,000 Harvard graduates would have only 50 descendants after 200
years if this continued, while 1,000 imported Italians would have multipli-
ed to 100,000. According to Terman, not only was a negro (genetically)
ignorant, but this also applied to most immigrants. Dutchmen and English-

men fared well, but according to the valid norms then, 83% of Jews, 80% of
Hungarians, 79% of Italians and 87% of Russians were mentally defective in
relation to the full-blooded American (whatever that is). It is self-
evident that neither psychologists nor politicians had anything good to say
about the qualities of the negro. Given the inequality of IQ, which reflects
the highest and most important human capability, social equality cannot
and should not exist. The result was the appearance of sterilization laws.
The "unfit" were described in a law that was passed in Iowa, as "criminals,
rapists, idiots, feebleminded, imbeciles, lunatics, drunkards, drug fiends,
epileptics, syphilitics, moral and sexual perverts and diseased and
degenerate persons". In 1931, 30 American states had these laws, and in
1945 this amount had considerably increased. It was also forbidden that
whites marry negroes, Chinese, Indians, Indonesians, representatives of the
Mongolian race, etc.[38].

    Immigration caused the government considerable uneasiness. In 1924 the
Johnson Act was passed, limiting this. A counter-movement consisted of
behaviourism (as stated previously) which, however, had little success.
The tide did not turn until about 1950 when the Carnegie Foundation, for
instance, ceased to finance eugenic research, and eugenic periodicals changed their names. It is, however, a misunderstanding to assume that the
social Darwinists and eugenicists died out. Crow[39] writes in 1969: "If
society decides to improve IQ by eugenic means, it will be useful in
providing estimates of the expected gain. I believe that we already know
enough to predict that a selection program to increase IQ or g would
work"[40]. Another contemporary psychologist whose opinions are in con-
junction with these, is Herrnstein[41]. He feels that profession and social
class are mainly determined by the hereditary IQ. This means that the
banishment of monotonous work will lead to many becoming unemployed because
they are too stupid to learn anything else. Thus, it is better to leave
the situation as it is, more so because the inclination to become unemployed works through in the family genes, which may be called an extraordinarily bold statement. Finally, in this context, we can also point to
publications of the professor in technical sciences, Shockley[42], which
have the same drift. Also, in European countries a contribution was made.
Sweden has known sterilization laws, and also doctors in The Netherlands,
laws or no laws, sterilized or castrated people for various reasons. The
culmination point was Nazi Germany. An example about the ideas which were
advocated by "intellectuals"[43]. The Germans adopted an absurd usage which

maintains that the blood has everything to do with heredity. They
considered the blood as the center of the person as well as of the nation.
Compare the Jehovah Witnesses who refuse blood transfusions, the Old
Testament prohibitions to consume blood, and the anthroposophical theory
of Rudolf Steiner, which says that "I" resides in the blood. We still
speak about having blue blood, to have royal blood, half and full-blooded,
blood relatives, blood brothers, and so on. The Spanish Castillian
families had a lighter skin and veins which shone through dark, so that
they spoke of *sangre azul* (also blue blood). Another misunderstanding is
the *telegony*. An ancient belief stipulates that a mare who mated with an
inferior stallion will never again give birth to "good" colts because she
had been infected forever, via the blood.

In 1919 a book appeared in Germany by A. Dinter (*Die Sünde wider das
Blut*) wherein it was remarked that the German blood was poisoned by the
blood of the Jews. The Nazi philosopher A. Rosenberg in 1934, reached the
limit with his work *Blut und Ehre* in which he states that the bloodsoul of
the German people should be kept pure. A quotation from a book by Bouterwek (1943) is enlightening. "Damals war Oesterreich noch weit vom Reiche
getrennt, das Land das im Geburtenrückgange an der Spitze stand. Eineiige
Zwillinge erschienen mir als ein ausgezeichnetes Mittel, von der Bedeutung
der Erbkraft zu überzeugen, die öde und unfruchtbare Milieugläubigkeit zu
widerlegen und rassenhygienischen Einsichten, die am Anfang jeder Bevölke-
rungspolitik stehen müssen, den Weg zu bahnen. Mit Hilfe eineiiger Zwillinge wollte ich zeigen, was die Umwelt kann - und wie wenig sie gegenüber
der Erbkraft vermag."

The rest of the history is known: sterilization, mass murder, the
breeding of Ariers, craniometry, deportation of people considered inferior,
"psychobiologische Verbrecherkunde", and so on. Sensational American
publications dating some ten years ago about the heredity of intelligence,
illustrate the perseverance of these ideas. Relatively few protests came
from Germany. They had known this all along anyway.

In view of the far-reaching social consequences which the manipulation
of the IQ has had during the recent history, it is time to ask ourselves
what exactly could be meant by intelligence. Some apects of the social
implications since 1945 will be considered in chapter 8 and 9.

Footnotes, Chapter 1.

1. See De Groot (1972)
2. Onians (1951), Snell (1955), also thanks to J.P.A. Stolk for the necessary material
3. Intellegere est visio quaedam
4. Compare - De mundi sensibilis atque intelligibilis forma ac principiis
5. Idea primum est, quod humanae mentis esse constituit
6. Nihil est in intellectu quod non prior fuerit in sensu ... nihil, intellectus ipse
7. See Van Parreren and Van der Bend (1978)
8. Kempthorne (1978)
9. Posthumus Meyes (1979)
10. Hunt (1961)
11. Lehrman (1953)
12. An instigator of this is the American biologist Wilson, whose book (1978) is well known. He and his followers have written about 25 books on this subject since 1971. A tangent plane in The Netherlands is the biological approach of criminal behaviour as advocated by Buikhuisen, criminologist at Leiden. For a sociobiological publication by a psychologist see Eysenck (1978)
13. See examples in Linschoten (1964)
14. In modern literature the age of 3 is mentioned as a limit. Piaget, however, is somewhat vague about the question concerning the relation between development and heredity. For a critical discussion of his work see Donaldson (1978)
15. According to Hunt (1961), however, there have been behaviourists who took the viewpoint that a child should not be stimulated too much, otherwise its development would be slowed down.
16. Urbach (1974)
17. Buss (1976)
18. Laissez faire, laissez passer, le monde va de lui même
19. Eysenck (1973)
20. Husen (1975)
21. Darwin's work is usually called the theory of evolution. For the sake of completeness it has to be stated that not all science theorists consider this name appropriate. Popper, for instance, feels that one cannot speak of a theory.

22. Blum (1978)

23. Rosenberg (1976)

24. Blum (1978)

25. Nelissen (1977)

26. As an example read Luria and Yudovich (1959)

27. Personal communication from Professor M. Nowakowska, Warsaw

28. Blum (1978)

29. Van Gent (1978)

30. See descriptions of his life and work Blum (1978), Burt (1962),
    Buss (1976), Van Hoorn et al. (1978)

31. Phrenology was invented around 1800 by Gall and Spurzheim. The idea
    was that a) psychic abilities had exact locations within the cerebral
                cortex,
             b) that the strength of these characteristics was reflected
                by the growth of a specific part of the cortex,
             c) that this led to bumps on, or dents in the cranium,
             d) that it was possible through craniometry to gain an
                understanding into the intellectual and emotional
                characteristics.
    Phrenology is nonsense.

32. See the next chapters for a further explanation of some statistical
    concepts. According to Galton's biographer Pearson, this connection
    with Quetelet is not entirely certain. See also Cowan (1972)

33. Allen (1975)

34. Van Hoorn et al. (1978)

35. Further we can name H.H. Goddard, R.M. Yerkes and R.S. Woodworth

36. Eysenck (1973)

37. Pastore (1978), Samelson (1977)

38. Van Hoorn et al. (1978)

39. See the article by J.F. Crow in the Harvard Educational Review of 1969.
    It is part of a series of reactions to a controversial article by
    Jensen

40. See chapter 5. The symbol h^2 concerns heredity and g is the so-called
    general intelligence factor

41. Herrnstein (1971)

42. Shockley (1972)

43. Montagu (1959)

2 WHAT IS INTELLIGENCE?

The question as to when a psychological term, which also belongs to common sense, possesses enough scientific status, is dependent upon the implicitely or explicitely employed science-philosophy. In physics, there was a time when the discernment of contingencies was aimed at, without knowing how and why they appeared. An example is Aristotle's theory of the force of gravity which basically holds that things, according to their nature, fall or do not fall. By registering the behaviour of objects it sometimes becomes possible to speak in terms of expectations. Some find this sufficient, others also wish to know *why* something does or does not occur.

The first viewpoint means that phenomena are placed into so-called operational definitions. Gravity means that a stone drops if it is let loose at a certain height, electricity contains that fresh frog legs suspended on an iron balcony will contract if they come into contact with a copper post, and temperature is what the thermometer registers. This form of scientific practice is restricted to viewing the phenomena and a possible assessment of coherence. Psychology has known a similar phase and some still proclaim this conception. An example is the "black box approach" of classical behaviourism (Watson, Skinner). We know enough about human behaviour if the important input-output relations are known; the question *how* behaviour arises is not important. Psychology is a science of prediction. Other schools do not agree with this and want to see the black box opened. This is true, for example, of so-called cognitivism which wants to advocate expectations about behaviour but, at the same time, wishes to explain and eventually control it. Within contemporary psychology, both visions (and gradations in between) appear, which can be demonstrated using the intelligence concept.

Part of the quarrels and misunderstandings of research workers rests on the implicit usage of various philosophies about the requirements which a theory of intelligence must meet. Blum[1], for example, says that intel-

ligence is an unscientific term because it cannot be defined. This sociologist adds that psychologists measure things which they cannot even
describe. These pronouncements are of little use because Blum does not make
clear at what point he feels that something is defined properly. In any
case, the problem that Blum broaches is important.

Definitions and reduction

In general, three definition stages can be distinguished. The first is
comprised of a verbal, intuitive description of a phenomenon. For example:
"intelligence is the ability to solve various types of problems". This
stage does not go beyond tautology. The second level is connected with the
possibility of measuring the phenomenon. Operational definitions fit into
this category. Electricity is the degree to which frog legs contract, an
electron is a nebulous trail in a Wilson chamber, and intelligence is what
this test measures. We now have constructed instruments that are capable
of making phenomena visible and to place them on a scale. Several sciences
were satisfied with more or less operational definitions. An example is
18th century physics which knew about 35 open and closed thermometers. They
were not only unreliable but often also difficult to compare. That problem
was solved by Fahrenheit who introduced the closed thermometer and devised
one scale. However, it was actually well into the 19th century before the
scale was theoretically supported. For this purpose it was necessary to
discover what heat was in general, loose from specific manifestations such
as the expanding and shrinking of matter in different degrees (Kelvin).
The second definition level, therefore, consists not of "reality" in
the sense of knowledge about the how and the why, but is limited to placing
the phenomena on a scale. This method of working is today still defended
by the hereditarians, such as Thorndike and Eysenck. Their premise is that
everything which exists, exists in certain degrees and can be measured. We
can measure intelligence with tests, therefore there is something called
intelligence. They refer, in this context, to similar statements from
physicists in the last century, such as Maxwell and Kelvin. The second
level also implies that, aided by measuring instruments, we can search for
relations with other phenomena and instruments. Intelligence is what this
test measures, but we would also like to know if the result has anything
to do with school performance, income, etc.
The third and last definition level assumes a theory about the *nature*

of the concept, plus the development of an instrument and the possibility
of using it to predict behaviour and possibly to change it. In the case of
intelligence, this means that we also know which process of a cognitive or
other nature, is related to problem solving and the like. Moreover, intellect can be measured, predicted and, if necessary or desired, be changed.
If possible, the latter should also be on a quantitative basis, that is, it
is not sufficient to state that, given a certain intervention, someone's
cognitive abilities will change in a given direction, but it also needs to
be stated to what degree and why the change occurs. This nuance within the
last definition level can also be found in eccnomics: a few decades ago it
could be predicted that under certain circumstances the savings quota would
change but the development of econometrics became a necessity to be able to
say *how much* the savings quota would increase or decrease.

Looking at the many descriptions of "intelligence", we encounter both
different definition levels and a reflection of theories and quasi-theories
about the origin of individual differences. Thomas Aquinas[2] spoke about the
ability to see differences in similar things and similarity in things which
seem different. This is a description of the verbal, intuitive type with
little pretension. Descartes[3] talks about the ability to judge, which is by
nature equal in all men. It is interesting here that the simplest definition
level is being utilized, while the philosopher does not appear to be
reluctant to make a statement about the distribution and the origin of the
phenomenon. Objections will be made stating that Descartes lived long ago
and that he, therefore, has not experienced the progress of psychology.
Unfortunately, however, contemporary literature does not offer much better.
Clearly et al.[3] in 1975, actually do the same as Descartes by explaining
that intelligence is the whole of acquired and applicable knowledge and
skills. Their standpoint about the origin of intelligence appears, at first
glance, to be the opposite, but the level of the definition is not higher.
Jensen[4] also operates on this plane by saying that intelligence refers to
a hereditary and general cognitive ability which can be seen as the highest
common factor of the requirements for solving multi-faceted problems.

For the sake of completeness, here are some more recent descriptions
which also provide little clarity[5]: the ability to think abstractly, give
a critical opinion, deal effectively with reality, the art of adjusting,
to be able to combine separate impressions, working with abstract symbols,
show insight into the relationship of things, learning ability, the ability
to formulate correct answers in terms of truth and fact, changeability of

the central nervous system, a biological mechanism to integrate stimuli
into organized behaviour, the ability to perceive, associate, imprint,
imagine, judge, and reason. In short, we are confronted with words - in
more or less modern jargon - which, in the form of sensory or non-sensory
connected knowledge, have been written down in philosophy for ages.

That history and progress do not coincide appears to be demonstrated
in 1972 by De Groot where he writes that intelligence is the skill to solve
rational problems. This is a circle because the terms intelligence and
rational historically, etymologically, and in content, are closely related.
However, there are stronger examples. Charlesworth[6] explains that intelligence is the disposition to be able to operate intelligently. Cronbach[7]
says that intelligence is a beast which everyone knows to exist but no one
has ever seen, a type of Loch Ness monster, but dwelling in the mind.
Mendel[8] tiredly decides that intelligence cannot be defined, so that little
else remains but the statement that intelligence is what this test measures.
Judging from definitions, intelligence theory has apparently not proceeded
much further than the frog legs and the 35 thermometers during Fahrenheit's
time.

Another criticism from Blum[9] is that intelligence tests measure to
what degree and how swiftly people are able to solve pointless puzzles,
whereas it should actually be about an entity that is linked to the solving
of important problems where productive mistakes are sensible and there is no
set time limit. The same is put forth by Lippman[10] who compares IQ tests
with an attempt to establish someone's athletic abilities by an hours
examination in the area of running, jumping, pulling, and throwing (which
may not be such a bad idea)[11]. Here we come to the so-called reduction
problem.

An example: Of Bruch's violin concerto it can be said that it is a
wonder of compositionary beauty. On the other hand, we cannot reproach the
cynic who explains that the piece consists of scraping horse-tails on cat
gut. Both descriptions are adequate, but take different aspects into
consideration. The reduction problem is related to the question as to what
does *not* need to be examined in order to still come to an interesting
conclusion, or rather, which factors that play a role in behaviour can be
excluded. A second aspect of reduction is that phenomena can be viewed in
more than one way.

A man falls down the stairs continually. He is sent to the oculist
who suspects that there is something wrong with the ability to see depth

with binocular cooperation. The oculist's test could consist of setting up
in his garden a large amount of stairs constructed with varying distances
between the steps, having his patient descend the stairs, keeping a check-
list of where he falls, and then calculating the depth threshold by using
the distance between the eyes, the distance between the steps, and the
patient's height. No oculist works in this manner because this threshold
can be sufficiently determined along the lines of reduction with a simple
vision test. That test is useful to the extent that it can describe and
predict behaviour on staircases, on the street, and a large number of other
situations. However, the moral is clear as day: not every test has, per
definition, proper validity.

For the time being, we must conclude that the definitions of intelligence are not on a very high level and provide little clarity. However,
it would be unjust to make a judgment on the grounds of descriptions only.
We will now go on to the measuring of intelligence.

Early Psychometrics

The first attempts to measure intelligence in one way or another were
made by Galton, McKeen Cattell, Binet, and Pearson[12]. As mentioned before,
Galton felt that simple sensory functions and bodily characteristics
reflected intellect. In spite of the fact that he combined 17 variables,
the correlations with "eminence" appeared to be far-fetched. Therefore, the
test had no validity, if we at least assume that "eminence" is related to
intelligence. In America, Galton had great influence on J. McKeen Cattell,
who in 1890 coined the term "mental test". He based himself on the same
presuppositions and worked with factors such as colour preference, auditory
acuity, reaction time, and so on. He attempted, through the use of the
correlation coefficient, which had been invented in the meanwhile, to say
something about school performance which was presumably related to intelligence. The first experiment was done in 1901 and had disappointing
results. The correlations between the researched factors were very low.
This seemed to mean that the test items were not inter-reducible. Moreover,
the correlations between the test and the school marks were about nil,
whereas that between school results themselves appeared to be relatively
high (about .60). Cattell, therefore, did have a test but could not get a
grip on intelligence, defined as an "ability" responsible for school
results.

About 1900, the Parisian physician Binet was pointed to the fact that many children could not keep up at school. The problem which was laid before him was whether they were too lazy or too stupid[13]. Together with Simon, Binet asked himself in which way these qualities could be separated. The goal was pragmatical. Binet was never interested in theoretical views about the background of school performance or intelligence. He contented himself with the search for a measure on the grounds of which children could be sorted by competence, according to their ability, and to place them in different types of schools. The "cause" of the differences between the children did not concern him. The sorting of individuals and the application of what can be called mental orthopedics, stood central (i.e. to give as many children as possible as many chances to be educated). Moreover, Binet did not see intelligence as an isolated factor but as something that contained links with personality as well as with social factors. He viewed the test result as an instance that need not point to stable qualities. The result served more as a guide for educational policy than as a means to make pronouncements about the future of the person involved.

Binet's first attempts were along the same lines as those of Galton and McKeen Cattell. He began with the inspection of faces and palm lines but soon found out that these features explained nothing. He decided to make tests in which the problems were related with matters that were taught in school. He devised questions in the area of the naming of objects, the completion of sentences, the understanding of simple stories, memory tests, providing definitions, finding similarities between objects, imitating gestures, listing words that rhyme, etc. Per test item, Binet and Simon endeavoured to establish and build in a successive grade of difficulty. The test scores were compared with school performance and it appeared to be possible to predict the latter quite reasonably from the former. In 1905 the first IQ test for selection purposes became reality.

If we look at McKeen Cattell and Binet's work, it is apparent that they, in view of the nature of intelligence, did not add anything of importance. McKeen Cattell's test did not work; Binet's predicted school success but this occurred by constructing a test which described, in a relatively trivial manner, what was taught at school. As mentioned before, Binet strived towards this, but McKeen Cattell still held that there must be something "within" the individual such as intelligence and that this ability was of a general and hereditary nature.

The stubborn presuppositions of McKeen Cattell et al. we also find in this time with Pearson. He asked teachers to estimate the "intelligence" of the pupils in their class on a seven points scale. Pearson allowed the teacher's fantasy to define intelligence. Pearson established that the correlation between children from the same family was approximately .50. He also found the same number with length (compare with Galton), state of health, and eye and hair colour. He viewed all of these as hereditarily determined and decided, therefore, that the same applied to intelligence. This conclusion must come as a surprise. Pearson also had no grip on the concept in question and, furthermore, correlations and causes need not be linked[14].

Three examples: Two watches are purchased and the correlation is calculated between the position of the hands at a number of arbitrary moments of observation. The correlation will be almost perfect, or rather, approximate the value of 1, but this does not say that watch A influences watch B, or that there is a secret force C which controls both, etc. The watches operate the same because they are similarly put together, but there is no relation that has something to do with influence. There is also a positive correlation between thickness of clothing and the chance of catching a cold. The remedy, however, is not that it is best to ride a hundred kilometers daily to work on a motorcycle in swimming trunks in the freezing cold. A third factor (in this case, the weather) is responsible for both the thick clothing as well as the inconvenience. A nice variant[15] is that the correlation between IQ and the number of missing teeth is -.63. The stupider you are the less teeth you have, but does this mean that intelligence improves the metabolism of tooth roots or that cavity-related bacteria exercise a secret influence on that part of the brain which produces IQ? The background of the phenomenon is presumably that people with a low IQ, on the average, have a relatively low income and have fewer possibilities to save their dentures with precious metals.

We see, therefore, at about the turn of the century, that excluding Binet and Simon, "theory" was more important than empiricism in regard to the concept of intelligence. Measurable or not, intelligence "exists" and is hereditarily determined. Still, it became bothersome that nothing further could be thought of.

Correlations, and then what?

The statistical relation between one variable and the other can be described by calculating the correlation coefficient. The number of possible (cor)relations increases rapidly with the number of variables under consideration. Since an important part of the social sciences consisted and consists of collecting thousands of correlations, it is therefore gratifying to develop techniques which can serve to describe these numbers. The most well-known methods in these area are path analysis and factor analysis.

Through path analysis, an attempt is made to unravel the correlation pattern in a scheme of "causal" influences. The strength of this influence is expressed, per variable pair, in a path coefficient. In the example of intelligence and defective dentures, it could apply that social status and dentures are connected by a path coefficient, just as status and intelligence, while the correlation does suggest this. We will return to this issue.

A second form of manipulation with correlations is factor analysis[16]. In short, this is aimed at locating general dimensions which lie behind many forms of behaviours. Actually, this description (which is encountered in most of the literature) is too euphoric, because factor analysis is only a relatively handy method to *describe* a number of correlations. The concept "dimension" suggests that out of the analysis a theory emerges about the how and why, and this is in no way the case. In 1938, Anastasi already had a sharp eye on that where she wrote[17]: "A 'factor' isolated by such analyses is simply a statement of the tendency for certain groups of behavior manifestations to vary concomitantly. It does not indicate the presence of any other characteristic or phenomenon beyond or beneath the concrete behavior." In other words: theory must precede factor analyses and not the other way around, whereby it can be noted that many do not appear to use this in practice.

Two examples are sufficient to do justice to the principle of the technique. A large group of children is gathered who attend primary school. They are selected in such a way that there is little variation in their report card marks, this means, therefore, that there are children with marks of 50 or 60 but also, over the whole group, those with marks of 80 or 90. They are given a test which consists of questions about what is learned at school: arithmetic, history, geography, reading, writing, etc. When everyone has completed the test, we correlate the calculations between arithmetic and history, arithmetic and geography, arithmetic and reading, history and geography, history and reading, etc. The correlations are placed in a matrix of 5 x 5, which produces therefore 25 correlations. Some of the factors have to be left out. It is useless to calculate the correlation between arithmethic and arithmetic, etc., which makes a difference of 5 correlations. Moreover, it applies that when we know how high the correlation is between test 1 and test 2, the same value is applicable for that between test 2 and test 1. This makes another difference of 10 correlations leaving us with a triangle of 10 correlations. In view of the manner in which these children are selected, it is to be expected that all the values are positive and high. Further analysis shows one factor upon which all the tests are highly loaded. What is now known, is that the results are related to one factor. Its name does not come rolling out of the computer, so that the researcher must make it up. An appropriate name is school success, but this was already known before.

On the occasion of a second experiment, a number of arbitrarily chosen adults are brought together. Tests are chosen on a very wide variety of areas, for example, solving quadratic equations, turning figures during a free fall in parachute jumping, writing down as many bird names as possible in one minute, singing Old MacDonald, adjusting a carburetor, running one hundred meters, modelling, and interpreting unclearly drawn pictures. Assume further that for every test, a scale is defined. The correlation matrix will now likely consist of values near nil and the factor analysis will produce as many factors as tests. The last is a complicated way of saying that the tests have nothing to do with each other. In other words: there is no indication that processes exist which clearly serve as a foundation for the result of more than one test.

In practice, situations are encountered which lie between such extremes. In secondary school, for example, it could apply that the correlations between the marks for foreign languages and those between the subjects in the area of mathematics, physics, and chemistry lay higher than those between languages and the mathematical subjects. Factor analysis could, in this case, possibly show two factors which could be called "language skill" and "mathematical insight". It is clear that these only say that school results seem to be related to two groups of marks. Whether language skill and mathematical insight may actually be *separated*, and which *processes* are involved here remains unclear. The latter is the danger of practising statistics in general and of factor analysis in particular without a proper theory.

One last example: an intelligence test is constructed with many diverse

questions. In alternation, the problem is posed asking whether general
Grant had to do with the war or whiskey (this is not an unrealistic type of
question), a series of numbers and sentences have to be completed, and
figures have to be recognized and copied. Furthermore, the subjects are
requested to multiply matrices, divide them, etc. Assume then that all the
subjects have learned matrix algebra and that they have been taught to
perform such manipulations numerically. The result of the matrix test will
then correlate highly with the number series, so that the researcher
concludes that matrix algebra is related to "thinking with numbers".
Another psychologist does the same but works with subjects who are used to
solving sums with matrices in a geometrical way. In this case, the
correlation with the figures could be high and the factor analysis exhibits
a high loading of matrix algebra on geometric thinking.

   This means that there is every cause for a violent as well as useless
argument between the researchers. The result depends on the *unknown* strategy
used by the subjects so that we once again see that factor analysis does
describe data but does not explain anything. The confusion becomes complete
when a third researcher does the experiment with victims where one-half
uses an algebraic strategy and the other half a geometric one. In that case,
the analysis "demonstrates" that this type of exercise is somewhat connected with both arithmetic and with geometric or spatial thinking.

   The moral is that factor analysis as such, does not provide a theory
and that it only serves to group numbers. What these groups *mean* is something else. Moreover, it applies that a number of types of factor analyses
(and axis rotation) can be used on one set of data which result in
different descriptions. Back to the theory about intelligence.

Vectors of the Mind

   Also with an eye to the intelligence problem, pre-phases of factor
analysis were developed in the beginning of this century by Spearman who
also founded a large part of statistics in general. He felt that school
performance and (primitive) tests reflected two factors which he named g
and s[18]. The first is an abbreviation of *general intelligence*. Spearman
assumed that it was an ability to discover relationships, more or less in
concurrence with Thomas Aquinas' definition of six centuries earlier. The
second factor stood for *specific intelligence*, that is, an ability to solve
various types of problems of which Spearman was not certain what they were

precisely related to. He hastily explained that this s factor was not very important. Spearman's view was strongly influenced by the theory to which he adhered. This contained that intelligence was a general and hereditary ability. He admitted to this boldly and made a plea for constructing tests in which the items were highly correlated so that, per definition, the factor g was measured.

Since Spearman, many tests have been constructed. Regarding various modern examples, Block[19] remarks that nothing has changed. The Stanford-Binet of 1960 has been initially designed by Terman and others who also thought that intelligence was g. In the handbook belonging to the test it is lightly written: "Tests that had low correlation with the total were dropped even though they were satisfactory in other respects." Block rightly concludes that it is not difficult to devise an intelligence test which indeed seems to measure g ("IQ tests have simply been *cooked* to have this property").

More or less elaborated forms of factor analysis became available in the thirties. Thurstone devised 56 tests which were administered to a group of 218 students. Using the method which was available to him, it appeared that the 56 were spread out over 9 factors. Therefore, he asked himself if it was useful to express intelligence in one number (IQ), and whether it should not be preferable to speak of an intelligence *profile*. Someone could do extremely well in working with numbers, be mediocre in language, have a very good memory, show reasonable spatial insight, etc. An extreme example of such a profile is the *idiot savant* (wise idiot), that is, someone who produces regular achievements but who demonstrates amazing qualities in one area (for example, mental arithmetic). A little later a discussion arose about the analysis techniques between Spearman and Thurstone, whereby the first was able to win the second over to the conclusion that intelligence actually consisted of a g factor with some marginal phenomena which reflected specific capabilities.

A few decades later, Cattell made the situation more complicated. According to him, intelligence consists of 17 factors. These rest, in turn, on a general dimension (a higher order factor) which Cattell again names g and which he splits into two components: *fluid* and *crystallized* intelligence. Cattell feels that the first could be best defined as the ability to learn, that is, a factor which has nothing to do with education as such but which does make it possible to benefit from education. This is supported by biological determinants, whereby we again come to the heredity of abilities of the mind. Test results, which could be explained from what was learned at school, were called *crystallized intelligence*.

In the sixties, Guilford went a step further. He devised 520 tests and concluded that people utilize 5 types of "mental operations" which are related to 4 types of "objects" and these are connected to 6 types of "mental products". Using multiplication, Guilford's theory comes to 120 independent (orthogonal) intelligence factors; he claims to now have empirically found about 100 of these. This material causes Elshout[20] to sigh that the number of "vectors of the mind" over the years, has only increased and that further growth can be expected if the psychologists make up more item styles. Elshout was not completely right because Guttman[21] presents, in 1976, three groups of variables and in the same year, Carroll[22] introduced 24 factors.

A well-known model is Jensen's[23] who again finds two factors. His ideas concur with Cattell's to such an extent that he speaks of type 1 and type 2 learning. The first is related to the ability of solving new problems of a complex nature; the second consists of things learned by heart and these rest on elementary operations such as associations. It appears that Jensen is informed of the work of the learning theorist Gagné[24], which has to do with the conflict between the so-called unitarianists and the pluralists in the psychology of learning. Unitarianism was devised by the behaviourists and says that all forms of learning, in man and animal, are based on one collection of laws. The pecking of a pigeon is a process which does not actually differ from that which plays a role in the solving of a differential equation. This idea is allied to intelligence as a *g* factor. On the contrary, Gagné counts himself as a pluralist, that is to the researchers who distinguish a *learning hierarchy* of 8 types of processes (from classical conditioning up to and including problem solving, whatever that may mean). These processes are related to not directly reducible mechanisms which, from a learning theoretical viewpoint, again make a plea for a multifactor theory of intelligence. However, in practice, the line is difficult to trace because correlationists and learning theorists avoid each other.

For the time being, we can conclude that the factor analysis based on research of intelligence has not produced a consensus. One of the reasons lies in the unknown strategies that people use on intelligence test items. Block[25] provides a number of considerations that are worthwhile. He sees theoryless psychometrics as "fictionalism" that cannot bring anything interesting to light. Part of the confrontation between the "factor schools" rests on the fact that various researchers have utilized diverse techniques which produce different outcomes. In this way, progress is possible until the year 3010, because in choosing method A or B a psychological reason is a necessity, and where this is lacking, we are committed to arbitrariness. As mentioned, a g factor can simply be found by selecting items until the test, as a whole, becomes homogeneous. Besides this, it is possible that sub-sets of a test are based on cognitive processes which overlap but are in no way identical. If one is not aware of these processes and, therefore,not of the overlap, parts of the test will correlate positively, but this does not tell us anything about g or something similar. Cronbach[25] points to a related score. "The usual high correlation between verbal and numerical abilities is due in part to the fact that persons who remain in school are trained on both types of content. If a culture were to treat map-making as a fundamental subject, then map-making proficiency, it is suspected, would correlate highly with verbal and numerical attainments." Here, two aspects are mentioned: intelligence could have a lot to do with schooling, and the test score can hardly be seen as apart from talents which are relevant in various cultures.

One of the multitude of intelligence tests is based on the art of drawing a person (the why of this exercise is unknown). Indian children appear to do this poorly and are consequently "stupid" in relation to whites, but the relation changes greatly when both groups are asked to draw a horse. Brody and Brody state that the "draw a man" test which, according to some, is culture-free, shows that Hopi Indians, on the average, reach an IQ of 124, while Arabs, who on account of their belief may not draw living beings, must be satisfied with about 60. Montagu[26] also provides such an example. A Mexican child is asked what would happen if his ears were cut off. The correct answer seems to be: "I would not be able to hear anymore" (which still is actually nonsense). The child's answer is, however: "then my sombrero would slip over my eyes", and that insight in the relation of things is then considered to be unintelligent. Daniels[27] mentions the other point made by Cronbach. The Stanford-Binet test asks children of seven and eight years old what they should do if they are on their way to school and realize that they will arrive late. In the handbook it stated that only answers wherein the term "to hurry" is implied, can be counted as correct. This means, therefore, that reactions such as "simply walk on and tell the teacher why I am late; do not go back,

etc." indicate stupidity. But from where do we receive the right to say
this? It is socially *desirable*, given our work ethos, to give such answer,
but does this ethical principle have anything to do with intelligence?

In short, we can continue to utilize factor analysis until we are blue
in the face; we should still know beforehand to what the stated questions
are *related* and certainly not make items which rest on what is socially
desirable. For that matter, Binet is an example of a researcher whose tests
were first made socially acceptable. He observed, in early versions, that
girls answered some questions more poorly on average than boys, after which
he changed the items in such a way that both populations came out the same.

Psychometrists and Cognitivists

To Piaget the conception is ascribed[28] that it is only of use to make
an inventory of differences between people when it is known which processes
lie at the bottom of these differences. According to him intelligence
research is aimed too much at developing what can be called selection
instruments, while it is much more important to know *why* someone gives a
correct or incorrect answer. Choice of type of schooling should not really
be made on the grounds of the test score but on the grounds of knowledge
about what the child can and cannot do and where differentiated forms of
education can subsequently be adapted. Today, Russian psychologists have
similar ideas[29], which has been shown by forbidding (intelligence) tests.
According to Vygotsky, the arsenal of possible cognitive operations which
is available to man is a condition for, as well as a result of, education.
This means that education should not follow what is called "the zone of
actual development" (the test), but should follow the zone of adjacent
development, whatever Vygotsky may mean here. Instead of psychometric test
research, emphasis is placed on connecting learning theory and educational
practice, as well as on the research of learning and thinking processes. An
informative book in this field is Resnick[30]. The text is simultaneously
tedious and interesting. Tedious, because many authors basically say the
same thing; interesting, in connection with other ways of learning more
about intelligence in the future. Almost all writers declare that something
has gone wrong in psychology. Already a century ago cognitivists and psychometrists opposed one another. The first group was led by Wundt et al. and
wanted to learn something about man, that is, about processes which occur
in the species whereby the individual was only seen as a random specimen.

Today the branch of psychology which supports this in general is experimental psychology. The psychometrists in particular came under the influence of
biology and, especially, Darwin's work. They were interested, for reasons
which were mentioned in chapter 1, in differences between individuals. From
the beginning, there has been a split between the process approach (the how
and why of thinking) and the psychometric point of view which mainly wanted
to describe, select, and predict. Thus, it was unfortunate that the
cognitivists were not interested in individual differences and the psychometrists rarely looked at the nature of measured processes. Tyler also
feels this, noting that one of the few exceptions within psychometrics
was Wechsler. In particular, the habit since the first World War to give
mass tests would have been fatal for possible mistake analyses and such.
Neisser emphasizes that daily experience is important and that the tests
are mainly involved with puzzles which are far removed from this, and he
again points out a cultural difference (see foregoing) by remarking that
Polynesians can navigate astonishingly well on the sea while on our IQ
tests they do very poorly. Goodnow adds some more examples of this.

An interesting article was written by Simon. He tried to program a
number of problems from IQ tests onto a computer, and attempted on the basis
of simulation to find out how and in how many ways a problem could be solved. An example is the tower of Hanoi.

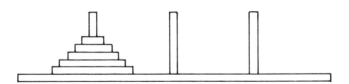

Figure 1. The tower of Hanoi

On a rod A there are a number of circular discs stacked in the shape of a
cone. It is the intention to bring the discs to rod B or C but with two
restrictions: only one disc may be moved at a time and it is not allowed to
put a disc on a smaller one. It can be calculated that the minimal number
of moves which are necessary to solve the puzzle is equal to $2^n - 1$, where
n stands for the number of discs. The example in figure 1, therefore,
assumes 31 moves. Simon proposed this type of problem to people. According

to him, there appear to be *four* rather fundamentally different strategies in finding the solution. Some of them are supported mainly by the short-term memory which can only store information for 20 to 40 seconds; other strategies have little to do with that memory. The strategy applied differs. Someone who is committed to his short-term memory can only solve the problem with a maximum of three discs. With a larger number of discs, another strategy or a combination is necessary.

The tendency of this example is the same as that of the matrices: to be able to say to what a test question is related, and what is meant by the term "intelligence", it is necessary to unfold cognitive strategies. Only at that moment is it useful to construct a test and to split and name possible factors. In the present situation, it is quite possible that the same test measures different things with different people.

Conclusion

The question that has been asked was: what is understood by intelligence? The answer depends on the definition which is considered acceptable. If it is required that a term reaches a high definition level, then there is hardly any idea of what intelligence is. That is very annoying for it means that we can stop. Therefore, we take a step backwards and go over to the internal definitions of operational thinking, that is, intelligence is what this test measures. As such, this is defendable to the extent that Fahrenheit's thermometer certainly did not rest on an adequate theory of heat, while it did provide services. The next questions, therefore, are, what are intelligence scores related to, how is a test constructed, and what can be said about the development of IQ from beginning to end?

Footnotes, Chapter 2

1. Blum (1978)
2. In: Jaspars (1975)
3. In: Urbach (1974), Cleary et al. (1975)
4. Jensen (1972)
5. In: Husen (1978), Resnick (1976)
6. In: Resnick (1976)
7. Cronbach (1970)
8. Mendel (1977)
9. Blum (1978)
10. Lippman (1975)
11. Compare chapter 21 of Wagenaar et al. (1978)
12. See Brody and Brody (1976)
13. Brody and Brody (1976), Blum (1978), Drenth (1975), Sarason (1976)
14. The philosopher Bertrand Russell has even made attempts to strike the
    term "causality" from the dictionary and to substitute it with (stable)
    functional relations or correlations. This can mean that at 12 o'clock
    the workmen in New York leave the factory "because" in Washington a
    whistle blows. Although Russell, on account of the problems which are
    attached to the term causality, had good arguments, this idea was still
    not adopted in broader circles.
15. In: Eysenck (1973)
16. Fruchter (1954)
17. In: Block (1976)
18. In: Brody and Brody (1976)
19. Block (1976), Cattell (1971), Guilford (1967)
20. Elshout (1976), see also Dumont (1972) and Dumont et al. (1977)
21. In: Resnick (1976)
22. Idem
23. Jensen (1972)
24. Gagné (1975)
25. In: Block (1976)
26. Montagu (1959)
27. Daniels (1976)
28. Furth (1973)
29. Nelissen et al. (1978)
30. Resnick (1976). The names which will be used further refer to
    authors of various chapters in Resnick's book.

3 TESTS AND WHAT THEY MEASURE

Although measuring and knowing are not the same, the first can cause
the second to blossom. A well-known measuring method in psychology is, of
old, the test. The word comes perhaps from *testa*, earthenware pot or melting
pot, a means to separate substances. The idea is that people do not randomly act everyday according to the situation but that they possess dispositions
to act, which are demonstrated in a multitude of circumstances, according
to a certain system. The need to learn about such inclinations is ancient[1].
In the Bible (Judges 17) Gideon thinned out an army by allowing the
frightened to retreat. The remainder drank water from a stream. Those who
did that by using their hands were regarded as watchful; those who layed down
were seen by Gideon as careless and unwanted. In the Middle Ages "objective
tests" made their entry on a large scale, that is, sorting methods which
rest totally on an intervention from the experimenter. The water-tight witch
tests became the best known. Further, bodily characteristics were chosen as
a point of departure to assess behaviour possibilities, such as skull knobs
(Gall and Spurzheim, phrenology), the face (Lombroso, Lavater), stature
(endless number of typologies such as those from Kretschmer and Sheldon),
and certain expressive devices such as handwriting (graphology). Extra-
terrestial factors (astrology) are already maintained for thousands of
years. All of this has contributed basically nothing.

The need for inventing instruments of measurement and scales upon which
qualities are placed and compared, presumably stems from psychiatry. Around
1800, Pinel wanted to settle accounts with the notion that the insane were
possessed by the devil. He felt that they only differed in degree from us
and attempted to state this by placing qualities in dimensions and to
demonstrate that individuals display the same properties in different
degrees. Shortly after Seguin applied this. He researched perception and
motion possibilities of the mentally deficient, and devised therapies for
them.

Near the turn of the century, personality and intelligence began to
be measured separately. In general, it holds that the test has not been
equally influential everywhere. Industrialized countries (England, America)
were the first; however, in Italy, Spain, Portugal, and Greece there was no
real development of any kind. The same is the case for countries such as
France and Germany. A possible reason here was that Mendel's genetics
assumed that discrete qualities were inherited. England and America were
influenced by behaviourism, which conceived man as a collection of
behaviours which were only moderately integrated and which could be measured
and described in a relatively isolated manner. This viewpoint which, on a
philosophical level, referred to positivism had little success in France
and Germany. Many psychologists advocated the so-called phenomenologist-
existentialist research methods, whereby the "total person" was studied on
an intuitive basis. This meant that "objective", and certainly mass tests,
were not highly regarded in opposition to projective tests (Rorschach), the
analysis of handwriting, and so on. In The Netherlands, this thought-climate
prevailed more or less till the end of the fifties.

Consequently, statistical techniques which have to do with test
construction and psychometrics in general (scaling, factor analysis, multi-
variate analysis), were mainly developed in England and America. In order
to be able to say something about tests and their construction it is
necessary to first look at simple statistics[2].

Measuring and Statistics

Measuring is described as the ascription of numbers to the phenomena
according to certain rules. Usually four levels of measurement are
distinguished.

In the nominal scale, the numbers indicate categories which have to do
with identifying something or someone. Examples are area codes and the shirt
numbers of soccer players. Counting is the only manipulation which is
relevant regarding content.

With the order or ordinal scale, numbers are connected to characteristics, whereby the magnitude of the differences and the zero point are not
known and/or defined. An example is a preference list of applicants; another
is the scratching of minerals on each other (scale of the geologist Mohs).
The hardest stone (diamond) scratches all other minerals and receives the
number 10, the second hardest is 9, etc. Here it also holds that manipula-

tions which go above the level of counting have no use.

The interval scale has fixed differences between the numbers, but the zero point is arbitrarily chosen. Examples are the temperature scaled of Celsius, Fahrenheit, and Reaumur. In this case it can be said that the difference between 20 and 40 degrees Celsius is the same as that between 60 and 80 degrees, but not that 40 degrees Celsius is two times as warm as 20 degrees. This means, therefore, that addition and subtraction are possible, but not multiplication, division, etc.

With the ratio scale, the intervals are defined and the zero point is not arbitrary. Each number on the scale is a certain distance from the zero point. Examples are length, time, and temperature in degrees Kelvin[3]. This scale offers room for many arithmetical manipulations.

The question asking to which scale IQ belongs depends again on the manner in which that concept is defined. The zero point of intelligence is, in any case, very difficult to establish, and if we adhere to higher levels of definition it also applies that we do not know how large the intervals between scores are. This should, therefore, mean that intelligence is placed on an ordinal scale, and even that might be saying too much.

Collections of numbers are described by calculating a central tendency. This can occur in many ways (mode, median, geometrical average, harmonic mean, etc.). Usually the arithmetic mean is chosen. The dispersion of measured values can also be expressed in many ways. The most well-known is the variance (s^2). Fo his goal, we take the arithmetic mean of a series ($\bar{x}$), establish the difference in relation to the average for all numbers, take the square of these values, add them up, and divide the sum by the number of observations (N). The variance is thus $s^2 = \Sigma(x - \bar{x})^2/N$. The standard deviation (s) is the square root of the variance.

Correlation is a technique to describe the statistical relationship between variables. Again, there is a large number of calculation methods available which differ in quality and which also depend on the measurement level. The product-moment correlation is most frequently used. This (r_{xy}) is $\Sigma\{(x - \bar{x}) (y - \bar{y})\}/Ns_x s_y$ where x and y represent both variables. The answer will lie between -1 and +1. Whether a correlation of .80 is twice as "strong" as .40 is a matter of definition. To be able to compare correlations they are squared, after which the percentage of described variance appears. In this example, the numbers have to do with 64% and 16% variance.

Correlation coefficients should be statistically significant, which means that they cannot easily be ascribed to coincidence. This depends

mainly on the number of pairs of observations. With thousands of observations, a correlation of, for instance, .05 could be significant, while .80
or more is necessary when there are only a few pairs. Note that the first
correlation might be significant, but that only 0.25% of the variance of
the measured values is described. Also, differences between correlations
should not be judged at first glance but should be tested. Here the same
applies in principle: with a large number of observations a difference of
.10 can be significant; with a small number this could very well be .50.
Correlation between two variables is called single, with more variables we
speak of a multiple correlation which can sometimes be dissected into a
number of single values (partitioning).

    Correlation is related to prediction. For that purpose a regression
line can be calculated in the form y = ax $\pm$ b. If the correlation is perfect
there is one regression line and y can be predicted with certainty on the
grounds of x and vice versa. If the correlation is 0, the points randomly
fill the space between the x axis and the y axis. It is then possible to
draw an infinite number of regression lines and we can predict nothing. A
clearer picture of this can be provided by drawing two regression lines
which run parallel to the x axis and the y axis. This means that on the
grounds of one x value we can expect y to be any value, and vice versa.

    If the correlation is imperfect, then there are, in principle, also
two regression lines. The one predicts y given x, the other predicts x when
y is known.

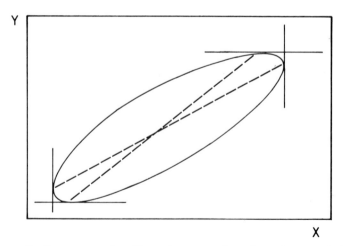

Figure 2. Two regression lines in case of an imperfect positive
          correlation

The outline of the scatter plot is drawn. This often resembles an ellipse. Four tangents are drawn parallel to both axes. Connecting the points of contact gives the regression lines. As the correlation decreases, the eccentricity of the ellipse increases as well as the angle between the lines. This angle is equal to $0.5\pi - 2 \arctan r_{xy}$ (rad).

The expected value of a variable is shown by a circumflex. Now it applies: $\hat{y}_x = r_{xy}(s_y/s_x)(x - \bar{x}) + \bar{y}$. Here $\hat{y}_x$ is the expected value of y, given x (the reverse, $\hat{x}_y$ may be written by the reader). Assume that $r_{xy} = .50$, $\bar{y} = 50$, $\bar{x} = 25$, $s_x = 5$ and $s_y = 3$. From this it follows: $\hat{y} = 0.3x + 42.5$. Thus if someone has a score x of 100, we can expect that y is equal to 72.5. The uncertainty of the prediction is hidden in r_{xy}. This means that the y scores do have an *average* of $0.3x + 42.5$, but that this value can vary. The degree in which this is the case is expressed by the standard error of measurement of y on x ($s_{y,x}$). This is equal to $s_y(1 - r_{xy}^2)^{\frac{1}{2}}$. In the example it holds that the y scores have an average expected value $\hat{y} = 0.3x + 42.5$ with a standard deviation of 2.6. Correlation and regression are related to each other. We can write $\hat{y}_x = r_{xy}(s_y/s_x)(x - \bar{x}) + \bar{y}$ as $\hat{y}_x = a(x - \bar{x}) + \bar{y}$, or $a = r_{xy}(s_y/s_x)$ and $r_{xy} = a(s_x/s_y)$.

A variable has a distribution. Mathematically, the number of possible distributions is infinite. In statistics, the so-called normal or Gaussian distribution (bell curve) is often used. If the successive powers of $(a + b)$ are written out and placed under each other, the so-called Pascal's triangle appears:

$$
\begin{array}{ccccccccccccc}
 & & & & & 1 & & 1 & & & & & \\
 & & & & 1 & & 2 & & 1 & & & & \\
 & & & 1 & & 3 & & 3 & & 1 & & & \\
 & & 1 & & 4 & & 6 & & 4 & & 1 & & \\
 & 1 & & 5 & & 10 & & 10 & & 5 & & 1 & \\
1 & & 6 & & 15 & & 20 & & 15 & & 6 & & 1 \\
\end{array}
$$

Note that a number in the triangle is equal to the sum of the numbers which lie above it on the left and the right. Let us choose the third line of the triangle which stands for $(a + b)^3$. Assume that a and b mean heads and tails and that we toss a coin three times. Define: $C_n^k = n!/k!\,(n - k)!$. The probabilities are then as follows:

0 times heads: $p_0 = C_3^0\left(\tfrac{1}{2}\right)^3 = 1/8$

1 times heads: $p_1 = C_3^1\left(\tfrac{1}{2}\right)^3 = 3/8$

2 times heads: $p_2 = C_3^2\left(\tfrac{1}{2}\right)^3 = 3/8$

3 times heads: $p_3 = c_3^3 \left(\tfrac{1}{2}\right)^3 = 1/8$

These are the same ratios which are in the third line. If this would be
done 8000 times then we expect 1000 times no heads, 3000 times 1 head,
3000 times 2 heads and 1000 times 3 heads. If the number of heads is set
out on the x axis and the number of observations on the y axis, a distribution appears. Herewith it applies that the mean is equal to $\bar{x} = pN = \tfrac{1}{2}N =$
$= 1.5$ times heads per toss with a standard deviation of $s = (pqN)^{\tfrac{1}{2}}$ where
p equals the probability tossing heads and q equals the probability of not
tossing heads, thus $s = (\tfrac{1}{2}.\tfrac{1}{2}.3)^{\tfrac{1}{2}} = 0.87$. If 100 coins were thrown each time,
the average would be 50 and the standard deviation would be 5.

The bottom line of the triangle is related to $(a + b)^6$. From the course
of the numbers it can be deducted that the limit $(a + b)^{\infty}$ gives a bell-
shaped distribution (see figure 3). The mean cuts the bell in two halves,
and one standard deviation lies under the inflection points on the x axis.
It can be calculated that the area between 1 standard deviation above and
below the average embraces 68.26% of the area; with 2 standard deviations
this is 95.44%; with 3 it is 99.72%. The limit of 100% is never actually
reached as the curve is based on an infinite number of tosses.

Assume that scores fit into such a "normal distribution". The
individual's score can then be transposed into the number of standard
deviations above or below the mean. These are z-scores. Someone who is 3
standard deviations above the average scores higher that 99.72% of the
population. With intelligence tests the agreed average is 100 and the
standard deviation is 15 (sometimes 16). Someone with an IQ of 145 (or 148)
therefore scores higher than 99.72% of the population. There are tables from
which we can read which area under the normal distribution is related to
varying z-scores.

The standard error of measurement is an indication of the reliability
of scores and has to do with the structure of the test. The error plays a
role in the estimation of result consistency of one subject. The standard
error of measurement of various intelligence tests lies somewhere between
3 and 5.

Assume that someone reaches a score of 95. We can then calculate how
large the probability is that this score is equal to or greater than 100.
The difference is at least 5 points, the standard error of measurement is
3, thus we find 1.67 standard deviations. The table shows that the area
outside 1.67s (the probability) comes to about 5%. Another question could
be how great the probability is that the score of John Smith with his IQ of

95 lies between 89.5 and 100.5. Here applies: 95 - 89.5 = 5.5 = 5.5/3 = 1.83
standard deviations, and 100.5 - 95 = 5.5/3 and thus also 1.83 standard
deviations. The area percentage under the normal distribution which falls
left and right from this is in total approximately 7%, which means that the
probability is 93%[4].

How a Test is Constructed

The way in which a test is constructed and the meaning of IQ differs
with children and adults. It is not precisely known what intelligence is,
but through daily experience everyone is aware of the phenomenon that
children, according to their development, as a rule improve more and more in
all kinds of areas. Performance can now be compared with the average of
one's peers. Assume that four test questions are devised. A correct answer
is +, an incorrect answer is shown as -. The following is then possible[5].

Age in Years	Question			
	1	2	3	4
6	+	+	+	+
7	+	+	+	+
8	+	+	+	+
9	+	+	+	+
10	-	-	-	-

A ten year old child is tested. The four questions have increasing degrees
of difficulty, and in such a way that an average six year old could answer
all the questions correctly at the simplest level. This child reaches the
performance of a nine year old. The IQ is the "mental age" divided by
calendar age times 100, or 90. In practice the results would be more dis-
ordered. An example:

Age in Years	Question			
	1	2	3	4
6	+	+	+	+
7	+	-	+	+
8	+	+	-	-
9	-	+	+	+
10	+	-	+	-
11	+	-	-	-
12	-	-	+	-
13	-	-	-	-

The candidate answered all the questions correctly which were intended for six year olds. To all the other correctly answered questions a mental age score of 0.25 year is given. The mental age is, therefore, 6 + 12/4 = 9 years and the IQ is again 90. The IQ of children is based on the average performance per age group and assumes the idea that there is a growth factor in intellect.

Various intelligence tests have shown that the scores of adults barely change in the course of their lives. This is partly caused by the nature of the questions asked. A mathematician, for example, will see his ability to multiply and divide quickly, reach a constant quite rapidly, but the boundaries of his knowledge will hereby no yet be attained. This phenomenon implies that one's IQ from year to year would become lower due to the fact that the denominator of the fraction increases irresistibly. That is strange and, therefore, the IQ of adults is calculated differently.

From a statistical viewpoint, it is handy to work with variables which are normally distributed. Fairly normal distributions are found if length or chest circumference of a large number of persons is measured. The experimenter is then limited to using a tape measure and a pencil. In order to find a normal distribution for intelligence, more is required.

Toss one hundred coins many times and tally the number of heads. Set the number of heads on the x axis and the percentage of the total number of tosses on the y axis. After a large number of attempts, a curve appears which very much resembles a normal distribution. Analogically, one can devise a hundred questions for an intelligence test in such a way that the probability of giving a correct answer is 50% and all correlations between the questions are zero. In that case, an approximately normal distribution will be found but this is of no use. The intention is (see chapter 2) that the test measures something "general" and Old MacDonald and quadratic equations have little to do with one another, so it is said. A second possibility is that the questions are again such that the probability of a correct answer over the population per question is 50%, while the correlations between the questions are 1. In that case, no distribution can be expected but only two points of measurement are found: half has everything correct, the other half everything incorrect. This test is, therefore, not capable of measuring small differences between people because the population falls into only two categories. The solution can be that not all questions are seen as having equal value but that a large number of levels of difficulty are built in with an *average* level of 50% correct and, moreover, that the questions are chosen in such a way that the intercorrelations are moderately positive. In this way a distribution will indeed appear which again resembles a normal distribution. The next step is to set the average at 100 and the standard deviation at 15 or 16, and to express the raw scores in standard or z-scores. Finally, the acquired standard scores are normalized, that is, the distances between the scores are stretched and reduced such that the whole is *forced* into a normal distribution. This means that 68.26% of the population *per definition* have an IQ between +1 and -1 standard deviation, i.e. between 85 and 115; that 95.44% have an IQ between 70 and 130, etc. The percentages are as follows:

IQ	%
145 and higher	0.14
130 - 144	2.14
115 - 129	13.59
100 - 114	34.13
85 - 99	34.13
70 - 84	13.59
55 - 69	2.14
54 and lower	0.14

Lastly, it is agreed that mental defectives have a score between 70 and 85, imbeciles score lower than 70, and that giftedness begins at 130. Galton's IQ of 200 lay 6.7 standard deviations above average. The chance of reaching this corresponds to approximately 10^{-11}, or rather a one-billionth percent and there have presumably been 10^{11} people. Therefore, Galton was indeed an extraordinary person.

The essence, in any case, is that a number of operations by the constructer of the test is necessary to allow the measuring of intelligence to adhere to a normal distribution. This is important for the following because some theories about the origin of differences between people say that intelligence and its distribution, just as length, is a *fact of nature*, from which conclusions are drawn. However, it is going too far to call the extent of a psychologist's thoughts a natural fact.

Figure 3 illustrates in which way various types of IQ scores relate to the normal distribution.

One of the simplest ways to describe raw scores is the calculation of percentiles. The population is set at 100% and is divided into 100 groups of 1% each. Thus, someone who is in the 90th percentile may say that 90% of the population scores lower, at the 60th percentile that is 60%, etc. The

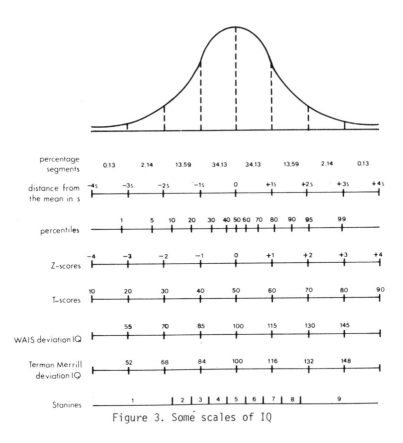

Figure 3. Some scales of IQ

percentile figures are set out on the horizontal axis, the vertical axis is a constant[6]. We can see in the figure how the rectangle fits into the normal distribution, as a result of which, for example, the distance between the 40th and 50th percentile on the x axis is much smaller than that between the 90th and 100th (the area under the distribution is the same). The WAIS scores refer to the Wechsler Adult Intelligence Scale with a standard deviation of 15; the Terman Merrill scores have a standard deviation of 16. In yet another scale (T scores) the mean is 50 and the standard deviation is 10. Stanines span a scale of 9 points, each a half a standard deviation wide.

Requirements of a Test

It is self-evident that a test must comply to more properties than the fact that the scores are finally normally distributed. An IQ test can be

defined[7] as an investigation of behaviour facets with the intention of
finding behaviour constants. For that purpose questions and exercises are
designed on the grounds of which it is possible to compare, on a
quantitative level, the characteristics of the person being tested with
those of others. The possibility of predicting behaviour is, however, an aid
and should not serve to take over responsibilities in making decisions. One
of the considerations to use a test is efficiency. Someone's intelligence
could perhaps be estimated in day-to-day life but then the right moment for
judging must be awaited. Moreover, the estimation will strongly depend on
what the observer feels is important.

This brings us to the item "standardization". The results must be
comparable to those of others which means that the test must be given in the
same situation, with the same instructions, identical material, same time
limit, etc. Accidental influences can never be completely avoided by this.
It is possible that someone, while writing down as quickly as he can, as
many kinds of birds as possible, has a sudden coughing fit, or gets something in his eye while trying to recognize poorly drawn pictures. Similar
effects can be more of a hindrance when many are taking the test than in an
individual test (the tester gives him another chance). Further, it is self-
evident that the test is "objective", whereby it is meant that the judging
of the correctness of the answer is not a matter that is subject to the
tester's mood. The test results must also be independent of the behaviour of
the one who establishes the IQ. This, for example, contrary to projective
tests such as the Rorschach whereby is seems to be possible to maneuver the
subject and therefore his personality in many ways by (unconsciously)
emitting sounds or raising the eyebrows with certain types of answers.
Different judges must reach the same outcome.

Reliability is also important. If the length of a number of people is
measured and placed in order, this order will be almost identical with
repeated measuring. However, with IQ tests this occurs less frequently. The
score is influenced by various situational variables and by the motivation
of the person at the time of the test, as a result of which a considerable
measurement error becomes manifest. This also occurs with repeated testing,
whereby an individual begins to display skill in performing certain
exercises (*test wiseness*).

Everything revolves around the validity of the test of which several
variants are named. The operational definition of intelligence places the
emphasis on predictive validity, that is, the test results must correlate

well with criteria such as school performance, profession, etc. Construct
validity implies that the test measures what it purports to measure (intelligence thus) and this is a weak point as it is not known exactly what
intelligence is about. Drenth remarks that countless definitions of
construct validity exist which seem to depend on the phantasy of the test
constructer. A third form is concurrent validity. This means that the test
must correlate well with other measurement instruments which are related to
the same. Van Peet[7] provides both a curious and illustrative example. In the
list of requirements that he places on the IQ test, the remark appears that
the test must show a connection to the teacher's opinion about the intelligence of the child. This seems to imply that the psychologist leaves the
defining of his concepts to laymen, which Pearson already did arround 1900.
Furthermore, Van Peet states that the test must demonstrate a connection
with performances for which *society* feels that intelligence is required.
Here the circle closes: do psychologists not know what intelligence is, say
(consequently) that "society" will know, and construct an instrument which
places uncontrolled inductions on a scale? This issue deserves attention.
But first something about the kinds of tests.

Types of Tests

Everyone knows that during the first years of life, children display
rapid growth in their behavioural possibilities. For the usual tests it is
necessary to be able to read and write. Tests for young children are aimed
at areas where knowledge of language is not needed. Various types of aspects
are chosen in perception and motor development (whether these factors have
anything to do with intelligence in later years is not established first).

Tests for young children are those by Gesell, the Cattell Infant
Intelligence Scale, the scales of Escalona Gorman, the Bayley, and the
WISC (Wechsler Intelligence Scale for Children). Tests for primary school
age are based on the work of Binet and Simon. Terman has made an American
version of that, the Stanford-Binet test of 1916, which has been repeatedly
revised.

During the first World War, the Army Alpha was given to many hundreds
of thousands by way of a group test, and used as a selection device for
functions in the army. The Army Beta was a non-verbal test and could also
be used to select immigrants who could read no English; the questions rested partly on pantomime. A while later, the tests of Wechsler followed, the

WISC and the WAIS (Wechsler Adult Intelligence Scale) and the Raven
Progressive Matrices, a non-verbal test which was presumed to be related to
the ability to reason logically and which is presented in The Netherlands
since the second World War to all those being selected for the military
service. The multi-factor theories of intelligence seem to have inspired the
DAT (Differential Aptitude Test) and the GATB (General Aptitude Test
Battery) which aid us in researching many factors which play a role in a
multitude of professions such as motor ability, adding and subtracting
figures, technical insight, word knowledge, spatial insight, etc. A seperate
case are the creativity tests which mainly rest on the work of Guilford and
partly consist of so-called open-end questions. This contains that some
possibility is suggested and that as many alternatives as possible must be
brought forward. Examples are: describe what happens if the force of
gravity would suddenly be halved, and list what a newspaper can be used
for. The amount and originality of the answers is called creativity. Lastly,
a few tests have been developed in the area of social intelligence. These
aim at solving problems which flow from interhuman contact.

In The Netherlands research about tests and the use of them only
commenced in the fifties and sixties. Presumably the reason was phenomeno-
logy, which had something against tests and experiments. The SON, the Snij-
ders-Oomen non-verbal intelligence scale, and the GALO (Groninger Afslui-
tingsonderzoek Lager Onderwijs), originated in 1958. The DAT was translated
in 1960 and in 1962 the GIT (Groninger Intelligentie Test) was constructed.
In 1966 a survey was carried out with the DAT in connection with performance
in elementary school. In 1968 Drenth et al. developed a test for children,
the AKIT, in 1969 a high-level verbal test followed by Van Wieringen, the
VAT, and in 1970 Drenth and Hoogwerf published two numerical tests, the
NAT. In that same year, the WAIS was translated. Kohnstamm made a language
test in 1971 (UTANT), and since 1973 attempts are made to construct social
intelligence tests. Also throughout the years school progress tests were
devised. At this moment as many as 63 tests are used on behalf of tests for
children in primary school, which include strange exercises such as drawing
a person.

Development of IQ

Many studies have been published which have been executed about the
changes in the course of life. The data can be divided for children and

adults. A scientific practitioner who enjoyed some renown was Einstein. He
could only speak a little at the age of three and it was assumed that he was
mentally deficient. At school his performance was moderate. He failed his
final exams in high school and also failed the entrance exams for the
Technical University. He just managed to make his Bachelors degree; only
after this did things start to improve. Approximately the same applied for
Darwin and Poincaré.

Apparently it is possible that intellectual growth follows an erratic
pattern. Van der Ven[8] mentions a study in which children between the ages of
4 and 12 years were regularly tested. One group remained fairly constant, a
second displayed a monotonic rise of IQ by as much as 50 points, and the
third dropped monotonically by as much as 30 points. Jensen[9] says that the
growth rate of intelligence is rather unpredictable, especially at an early
age. This also applies to height, which is one of his arguments in viewing
intelligence as being hereditarily determined. Intelligence, height, muscle
strength, and weight become more stable from school age onward in the sense
that the correlations from year to year come out higher.

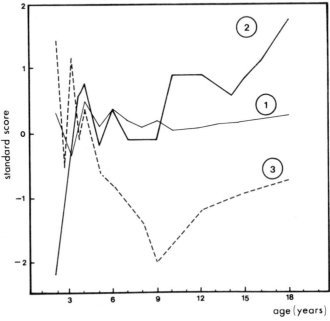

Figure 4. Results of three children in repeatedly taken intelligence tests

Sir Cyril Burt[10] assumed that IQ reflected the factor g and consequently was fixed at the outset. Lewis contests that. Especially with young children very low correlations are found from year to year. He even mentions a correlation of -.30 with IQ at the age of 16 to 18 years. McCall et al.[11] say that children between 3 and 12 years on the average show a variation of 24 points, with extremes up to 60 points. Cronbach[12] shows a picture with three types of changes between 3 and 18 years. Figure 4. Case 1 is stable, 2 exhibits an increase over the years, and 3 shows an erratic course. To what extent emotional and intellectual functions are interwoven is apparent with child 3. When she was 9 years old her mother remarried and the child felt very uncertain. The moral here is clear: making predictions on the grounds of one or even various observations can be an extremely critical undertaking, especially with children.

An important longitudinal experiment is the Berkeley Growth Study[14], connected to the vicissitudes of 61 people who were born in 1928 and 1929. The following table shows correlations of various ages with IQ at the age of 17 and 18 years.

Age	Correlation
months	
1 - 3	.05
4 - 6	-.01
7 - 9	.20
10 - 12	.41
13 - 15	.23
18 - 24	.55
27 - 36	.54
42 - 54	.62
years	
5 - 7	.86
8 - 10	.89
11 - 13	.96
14 - 16	.96

A number of points catch the eye. Up to school age the correlations are low. At 13 - 15 months, for example, only 5% is described of the variance of 17 and 18 year olds. Besides, no pattern can be distinguished in the correlations so that there are no indications of monotonic growth or something similar. This again means that the prediction of later IQ on the basis of tests for children is almost impossible. Various explanations can be thought of here.

It is possible that "true" intellectual growth passes capriciously until school age is reached. An alternative is that the tests for the different age periods are incomparable, for example, in the sense that sensory and motor tests for young children have little to do with what we later call intelligence. Firstly, it is not simple to make a choice. Moreover, it makes little sense to speak of "true growth" if the matter at issue is unclear in itself. The conclusion is apparent that it is not known which processes with young children possibly lie at the base of IQ.

In a textbook about developmental psychology, Mönks and Knoers write that 20% of IQ is fixed at the age of 1 year, at 4 years 50% is formed, and at the age of 8 years 80%. It is striking that this passage contains three errors. If it is said that something has attained a certain percentage of the final stage, measurement on the level of a ratio scale is assumed, and few dare to state that regarding intelligence. In the second place, the authors should have mentioned percentage *variance*, and in the third place the given values are incorrect. It can be seen in the table that IQ suddenly does become reasonable predictable from school age on. A simple reason can be that IQ and schooling are related, an issue that must also be looked at.

Apart from correlations it is also interesting to calculate other things. When the IQ of 6 month old children is compared with that of elementary school age, it appears in this growth study that the difference between the highest and lowest value is 58 points. The average change is 21.6 with a standard deviation of 15.7. In time the variance decreases fairly monotonically; at the age of 14 years the average change is still only 5.8 with a standard deviation of 4.7. What does this mean? Many draw the conclusion that compensation programs are only useful if they commence at an early age, that is, at a time when the nervous system is still "plastic". This conclusion is debatable. Predictability and changeability do not have to be related, and the pronouncement stands on shaky territory because it is unknown what intelligence (with children) exactly is.

There are indications[14] that cognitive growth correlates positively with the previous level. This should mean that those who ultimately score high have shown the greatest increase at the outset. The correlations are not influenced by this phenomenon because the relative positions of individuals remain the same over time. Intelligence must exist from "something". If these factors, of whatever nature, have a constant influence there is no single reason to assume that one period in life should be pre-eminently suitable to influence the process. Only if the development of intelligence is connected to so-called "critical periods", should (early) interventions be preferred[15].

Another longitudinal study[16] mentions that from 10 years of age the correlation with intelligence of the adult is approximately .75. Others[17] notice an average change of 20 points with adults who were followed for 20 years and tested every 5 years. Sometimes extremes emerged to as much as 70 points. McCall et al.[18] also contend, in this context, that high correlations can easily go together with large fluctuations of the group average, and that a high correlation need not necessarily imply stability alias unchangeability of intelligence. The influence of child-rearing variables is suggested, according to them, by the higher correlation of IQ with the mother than the intelligence of the father. However, in various studies, such a difference has not actually been found. The picture becomes still more complicated when multi-factor theories are studied. The language skills of girls when they are one year old would correlate .74 with the verbal IQ at the age of 26, while this correlation with boys is nil[19]. Any explanation is non-existent.

A part of the problem related to (the interpretation of) the unpredictability of intelligence with young children[20] can simply lie hidden in the low correlations between the children's tests in relation to one another, such as those of Gesell, Bayley, Escalona Gorman, Uzgiris Hunt, etc. With children of 14 to 22 months the correlations between the Bayley and various scales of the Uzgiris Hunt test lie between -.35 and +.54 which causes us to think of a weather forecast which says that the temperature for tomorrow could lie between -20 and +20 degrees[21]. It is of little use to list many of those figures; the average is somewhere in the area of .20 to .30. This means that not only a firm hold on later intelligence is missing, but also that at an early age, depending on the chosen test, we are basically groping in the dark.

Concerning the studies about the changes of IQ with adults, longitudinal data as a rule are also in disagreement with transversal data. Longitudinal means that one group is studied over time and, thus, is tested repeatedly. Impatient researchers determine IQ with a large amount of age groups at the same time (transversal). As a rule, longitudinal studies show that IQ up to the age of about 65 remains fairly constant; transversal studies often demonstrate a decline from 40 years. Some[22] have combined both approaches and find the same difference, in that respect that it would be incorrect to speak of "the" IQ. The scores fluctuate sharply per subtest, that is, spatial insight and verbal reasoning can exhibit an erratic course.

An obvious interpretation of the data is that with the transversal study
one test is used to determine the IQ of people between, for example, the
ages of 20 and 80 years, that is, people whose nature of schooling is highly
varied, with the result that the test with the one group embraces education
much more than with the other. A rather trivial fact is that those who,
during a period of 5 to 10 years, demonstrated a sharp decrease of IQ,
appeared to have an increased mortality rate. That applied mainly for old
people; we may thus fear that artery calcification and other degenerating
diseases which affect, among other things, the nervous system, have something to do with intelligence scores.

Occupation, Schooling, Income, Creativity

It was stated earlier that one of the requirements of an intelligence
test is that behaviours are measured for which society feels one should be
intelligent. It would be incorrect to ridicule this statement as this raises
an interesting issue. Jensen[23] remarks that intelligence must not be seen
as belonging to God-given desiderata, but that we are speaking about a
construct which reflects the value priorities in *our* culture (compare this
to the Indian children who could draw horses well, the outstanding Polynesian
navigators, etc.). Every society has its own preferences[24]. With hunting
peoples perceptual sharpness and archery are more important than completing
sentences. With us the emphasis lies on working with verbal and numerical
symbols, but that is a matter of choice, and as such we can see that
differences between races and cultures might exist.

There is a correlation between IQ and professional level, whereby it
applies that most shrimp peelers score lower than the average professor.
This correlation naturally rests on a certain ordering of professions; if
unskilled labourers would be put at the top of the list and we refer
professors to the bottom, the correlation with professional ordering is
negative, and it will be nil if we list the professions randomly. Apparently
the prestige of profession and IQ are related. The correlations between IQ
and the educational level (again such a scale) and school marks lie in the
area of .50; correlations with years of schooling is approximately .70, and
education again correlates positively with professional level and income[25].
Therefore, the higher the IQ, the more schooling and a higher socioeconomic
status (SES) one has. Others[26] report that the correlation between IQ and

profession is .46, between intelligence and school performance it would be
.58, and the correlation between school performance and professional level
is .63. The multiple correlation between professional level, intelligence,
and educational level is .64, no higher that that between the professional
and educational level. Husén concludes that we do not know how this network
should be unravelled, or rather what should lay at the base. On the grounds
of the same factors, various researchers defend various causal models.
According to Husén, income is mainly determined by "luck", because
irrespective of education and profession, IQ and income only correlate .13
which does not describe more than 1.7% variance. He concludes that cognitive
differences hardly relate to "economic success". The connection between
intelligence, profession and income would mainly arise via the educational
system and the opportunities received in that area. Education leads to a
diploma that has a "credibility effect". Psychologists are paid well because
they have their doctorate, and not in the first place because their intellect
has reached an immense value.

Also relevant here is a study by Duncan et al.[27]. The researchers made
a list of 120 occupations and asked their subjects (psychologists) to
estimate the IQ necessary for each occupation. Besides this an order had to
be made in the list by using the concept "status". The correlations were
somewhere between .80 and .90. The authors conclude that what psychologists
think is intelligence is connected with the idea that we have about social
prestige, and the last has to do with education and income. The correlation
between IQ and occupation could thus ordinarily emerge because psychologists
construct tests on the basis of social norms. Blum[28] adds cynically that
alcohol consumption correlates .50 with income and profession, from which it
could be naively concluded that especially heavy drinkers do well. Duncan et
al. conclude: "Our argument tends to imply that a correlation between IQ and
occupational achievement was more or less built into IQ tests, by virtue of
the psychologists' implicit acceptance of the social standards of the general
populace."

Also, these authors have attempted to unravel the web of correlations.
The conclusion is that IQ and occupation hardly have anything to do with
each other and that educational opportunities take the central position[29].
They report that the correlations between IQ, occupation, and level of
schooling are all about .50. If the correlations between IQ and schooling
and between schooling and occupation are excluded, the correlation between
IQ and occupation would be about nil. Some[30] use this to say that society is

hierarchically ordered, whereby schooling takes the central position. This
hierarchy would produce the test differences and these, in turn, are
utilized to maintain the hierarchy via selection.

Finally, a survey by Bowles and Gintis[31] is important in this context.
As we saw with Spencer and Galton, the poor are poor because they are
stupid. The latter is genetically determined and lies at the base of
success in life. The result is, therefore, that the class structure
inevitably reproduces itself, just like death and taxes. This viewpoint is
defended nowadays by adherents of the nature theory relating to intelligence
differences, such as Eysenck, Jensen, and Herrnstein. Bowles and Gintis
contend, in short, the following:

Make a table with IQ in deciles and economic success, also in deciles.
The correlation, according to them, is .52. If someone is chosen who qua IQ
belongs to the highest decile the chance that he also belongs to the highest
economic decile is 3.09 times as great as can be expected according to
chance. With the same comparison of schooling versus economic success, the
effect is stronger; in this case we find 3.76. With social class and
economic success we find 3.26. Therefore, at least three variables play a
role. For Eysenck et al. the structure of this poses no problem: IQ is the
foundation of economic success as well as of schooling, and IQ is mainly
inherited, which means that people with a high score probably also originate
from the higher social strata of the population. Bowles and Gintis apply
linear regression analysis to the material, and they then ascertain the
following:

Although there is a correlation between IQ and economic success, IQ
does not contribute greatly. The correlations would rest on the fact that
the variables have to do with the social class to which the child belongs
and the schooling. In the second place, they conclude that although there
is a correlation between schooling and economic success, the latter is only
slightly determined by the intellectual abilities which are acquired at
school. In the third place, the authors mention that economic success is
mainly connected to family circumstances and that IQ scarcely has an effect.
In other words: according to them, the social classes are reproduced via
mechanisms which have little to do with heredity, and the acquisition and
rewarding of intellect. This can also be stated in another way. Given the
social background and the schooling, IQ differences are not important for
economic success. There is a relation between IQ and economic success, but
if people are chosen with the same social class and schooling it appears,

according to them, that the correlation is a product of social influences. A variant of this is to select people with the same IQ and then look at the effect of schooling on economic success. With identical intelligence and divergent schooling, it appears that the latter has much to say about income and the like. Therefore, schooling is important, but its influence must be of an almost non-cognitive nature because IQ contributes little. Finally, we can compare tables about social class and IQ, as well as economic success and class, given a certain IQ. These tables are virtually identical. The authors conclude therefore that IQ and schooling are, in the first place, related to the social class from which one originates, and that *this* factor is mainly responsible for occupation and income. Other surveys, however, differentiate this rather extreme proposition (see chapter 9).

Irrespective of the correlation between IQ and occupational level, we can also look at the relation between intelligence and success within an occupation. In itself this is quite realistic because the practitioners of, for example, academic occupations show a difference up to 50 IQ points. The correlations[32] would not actually be higher than .20; others[33] claim that this figure lies in the area of nil with many occupations. The dissatisfaction with an occupation would, however, correlate positively with IQ. Drenth[34] draws attention to the gigantic differences which have been encountered here. The correlation between IQ and occupational success in the administrative sector lies between -.40 and +.80. With engineers a test for spatial insight correlates between -.55 and +.65. Consequently, the author takes the standpoint that between 1920 and the present nothing has been gained regarding the predictive validity of intelligence tests. He names, among other things, the lack of theory construction as a cause of this. Hoyt[35] looked at 40 surveys about the correlation between school achievements, IQ, and success within the occupation. According to him, these lie between -.07 and +.13. Therefore, they mean nothing.

Still another question asks what intelligence has to do with creativity. The selectivity of that which is measured by IQ tests appears from the fact that IQ and school achievements have little to do with artistic and social qualities[36]. A problem is that it is not exactly known what is meant by creativity. If we say that creativity is what this test measures, in any case a few differences with the IQ test will be apparent. With an intelligence test only one answer is correct and nothing new needs to be thought up, the time limit is short (if this is left out, the

differences between people become much smaller), and the test is concerned
with a large amount of small problems, while creativity would center on more
difficult issues. Especially Guilford devised tests which rest on the open
end questions mentioned earlier. The correlation with IQ is, in any case,
not high and the predictive validity slight[37]. Longitudinally[38], creativity
tests correlate only .40 with themselves. Only with salesmen there is a high
positive correlation between creativity scores and occupational success.
Thus, we are concerned here with people who must be able to fabricate many
arguments to be able to sell anything[39]. The researching of creativity is
developing rapidly. As a reason it is said that IQ tests have failed and
that our complicated society not only needs problem solvers but also, and
mainly, inventors[40].

What is the use of the IQ Test?

Looking at the discussed material, there is reason to ask the question
why intelligence tests are actually still being developed and used. The
processes involved lie for the most part beyond the horizon. About the
development of intelligence with young children little can be said, and
with adults education seems to be central. The interwovenness of IQ and
schooling appears, amongst other things, from the fact that recruits between
the two World Wars scored as much as one standard deviation higher[41].
Relations are scarce between IQ and success within the occupation,
creativity also seems to have little to do with intelligence, and the
correlations with occupational level, schooling, and income can be interpreted in various ways.

Van Putten and Rijnbeek[42] report that in the framework of elementary
education, many devices are tested to select children, such as the IQ test,
the school progress tests, experimental classes, and entrance exams.
Longitudinal research points out, according to them, that the best
predictors of school success are, respectively, opinion of the principal,
school progress tests, the IQ test, and the social class from which the
child originates. The great importance of the teacher's judgment means a
disqualification of the test, because the advice does not improve if one or
another test (out of a collection of 63) is also taken. The principal of the
school feels that he can state a sound expectation of the future for 75% of
the pupils, a psychologist can do this with 70%, and what is more important,
in 75% of the cases the psychologist and principal recommend *the same*.

Consequently, the moral of testing for selective purposes at primary school seems to be lost, and we have no indications that the IQ test renders important services in another context. Herrnstein remarks somewhere that the intelligence test is one of the most beautiful instruments which psychology has produced. It is nice to know that pessimists are amongst us[43].

Footnotes, Chapter 3

1. Drenth (1975, 1976)
2. For more information see Cronbach (1970), Drenth (1975,1976), and Hays (1977).
3. The latter is questionable, however, because the Kelvin scale seems to relate logarithmically to the kinetic energy of the particles of matter which is held responsible for heat.
4. For the sake of simplicity it is (unjustly) assumed that measurement error is always normally distributed and is equal over the complete scale.
5. From Drenth (1975)
6. Other methods are deciles (10 equal groups) and vigintiles (20 equal groups).
7. Drenth (1975), see also Van Peet (1974)
8. Van der Ven (1976)
9. Jensen (1972)
10. In: Lewis (1973)
11. McCall et al. (1973)
12. Cronbach (1970)
13. Jones and Bayley (1941), see also Mönks and Knoers (1978)
14. Pinneau (1961)
15. We will return to this in a later chapter.
16. Magnussen and Backeteman (1977)
17. Tyler (1972)
18. McCall et al. (1973)
19. In: Brody and Brody (1976)
20. For an overview see Brody and Brody (1976)
21. King et al. (1973)
22. Schaie and Strother (1968)
23. Jensen (1972)
24. Husén (1975)
25. Brody and Brody (1976)
26. Husén (1975)
27. Duncan et al. (1972)
28. Blum (1978)
29. Also see chapter 6.
30. Lewis (1973)

31. Bowles and Gintis (1972-1973), also see Halsey (1958) and Eckland (1967)
32. Duncan et al. (1972)
33. Brody and Brody (1976)
34. Drenth (1975)
35. Hoyt (1965)
36. Holland et al. (1964), Brody and Brody (1976)
37. Holland (1972)
38. Magnussen and Backeteman (1977)
39. Baird (1972)
40. Blum (1978)
41. Van der Ven (1976)
42. Van Putten and Rijnbeek (1978)
43. Those who wish to do an IQ test (or sections of one) should see
    Bernard and Leopold (1962).

4 REGRESSION TOWARD THE MEAN - A MYSTERIOUS FORCE OF NATURE?

There is a number of theories about the origin of intelligence differences. The most familiar are the genetic (nature) model, the environmental (nurture) theory, and a notion which says that the combined action of nature and nurture is responsible. The latter is closely related to the viewpoint of the hereditarians. All of these have to do with a strange statistical phenomenon. It is known as regression toward the mean. Strictly taken, egression away from the mean must be added. Adherents of the various viewpoints have to do with or appeal to the phenomenon, so that it is useful to discuss this. Three forms must be distinguished: regression within the individual, regression with repeated measuring within one group, and regression over different groups[1].

Regression Within the Individual

Instructors who were linked to a training center for pilots discovered a pedagogical law a few years ago[2]. In learning to fly it seemed that the most important difficulty was to make soft landings. The roughness of a landing can be placed on a scale and the scores will likely fit into some distribution. The instructors had observed that rewarding a pupil who had made a very soft landing was often followed by a rougher landing, and the reverse, that punishing rough landings often led to a better performance on the following try. The "law" read as follows, that performances were stimulated by being cross at stipulated times, and were thwarted if a friendly attitude was taken towards the student.

Some are never allowed a bright moment. The landing is determined by a large number of factors which could work for or against. With the latter we can think of a sudden gust of side-wind, lack of sleep, just missing the throttle at the critical moment, a bump in the runway, and being overcome by a bout of sneezing. In scoring a large number of landings, a certain

average performance level becomes apparent that will improve in time, but
now and then positive and negative extremes occur. These are caused by the
fact that the diverse factors which play a role sometimes all work with or
all work against, but statistically this is unlikely. Repetition of both a
very rough landing as well as a very smooth one is, therefore, not often
expected, which was wrongly interpreted as a result of a pedagogical
principle. In general, it applies that some performance which rests on the
action of a large number of (independent) factors alternated, and that the
probability of a very high or low score is quite small. In other words:
after an extreme result the next attempt will likely point more in the
direction of the personal average (regression). In the reverse, someone can,
after scoring in the neighbourhood of his mean, show a large improvement or
deterioration (egression).

Repeated Measuring of One Group

It can be presumed that the same occurs with the intelligence test.
Coincidence, concentration, motivation, etc. also occur here. This means
that when a number of people are selected with a very high IQ, 160 for
example, and are tested again, the average of the group will come out
slightly lower, and the reverse, that those with a very low score will
reach, on the average, a somewhat higher level.

The same or a comparable IQ test is given two times to a group of
school children, separated by a break of a number of weeks or months. The
test-retest correlation is (also) dependent on the lenght of the interval[3],
but often lies in the neighbourhood of .60 (see chapter 3). Assume that
both tests are normalized at a mean of 100 and a standard deviation of 15.
A group of children is chosen who all scored 70 on the first test. It now
applies that their distance from the mean in the retest will decrease to an
average of $100 - (0.6 \times 30) = 82$. With identical means and variances, the
regression is equal to the value of the correlation times the distance from
the mean on the first test. Or: $\hat{y}_x = r_{xy}(s_y/s_x)(x - \bar{x}) + \bar{y}$, or rather:
$\hat{y}_x = 0.6(15/15)(70 - 100) + 100 = 82$. Thus, it is expected that these
children, on the retest, will have an average of 82 with a standard
deviation of $s_{yx} = s_y(1 - r_{xy}^2)^{\frac{1}{2}} = 12$. In terms of probabilities this means
(see the table in chapter 3) that in percentages, $34.13 + 34.13 + 13.59 +$
$+ 2.14 = 83.99\%$ shows a "profit" of 1 IQ point or more; $34.13 + 13.59 +$
$+ 2.14 = 49.86\%$ increase 12 or more points: $13.59 + 2.14 = 15.73\%$ go up 24

points or more, and 2.14% "earn" as much as 36 points or more and go, therefore, from mentally defective to above normal. The reverse also holds. From a group of children with an IQ of 130, 2.14% decrease by 36 points or more on the retest and fall, therefore, from a talented to a sub-normal level. An example of the latter is a survey by Terman about the course of life of intelligent children. He started with a group which had an average IQ of 151. A number of years later the mean on a retest appeared to be 133. The test-retest reliability increases with age and in this case was approximately .70.

This phenomenon is a result of the imperfect test-retest correlation and there is not much that can be done about it. With programs which are geared to increase IQ, the phenomenon can play an annoying role. Assume that the group with an IQ of 70 is chosen to participate in such a procedure. In the course of time, a considerable improvement is encountered, but this does not necessarily have anything to do with the program and would have occurred anyway if nothing had been done with the children, or if they had been given a "learning pill" or had been ordered to eat french fries everyday. A comparable control group is, therefore, an urgent requisite, but also in this case something can go wrong.

Assume the following. A psychologist observes that children from a social middle class have an average IQ of 100, while this value for a lower class is about 80. He decides to choose children with an IQ of 80 who come from *both* groups; the middle class forms the experimental group, the other the control group. The results will probably indicate that the experimental group has improved (presumably to an average of 88), while the others stayed the same (80). The positive effect of the operation can entirely be ascribed to regression toward the mean. A second variant is that he chooses the children from the lower social class as the experimental group. Assume that the program does not work, but that the experimenter is not aware of this. After some time the experiment seems to have been done for nothing because the average is still 80, while the control group has increased their average to 88. The conclusion could then read that compensation programs do no work or are even detrimental and that intelligence is hereditarily determined (or so), because the children from the middle class continue to improve without special measures. When *both* groups would be exposed to the program and the operation is useless (again), the same will occur. The conclusion can then be that compensation programs have no use in so far that only children from higher social classes benefit from them (see chapter 8).

It sounds improbable, but errors of this type have been made repeatedly[4] and the background is obvious: it is hazardous to select individuals on
the grounds of extreme scoring in relation to the population average. Of
course, there are various research set-ups wich can deal with these kinds
of artifacts[5]. The simplest is that groups are composed on the basis of
large samples which have been randomly drawn from various populations after
which the individuals are randomly distributed over the experimental and
control groups.

The phenomenon in question is related to imperfect correlations.
Correlations give no information about causal relationships, at least not
without further analysis. Consequently, regression does not fit, per
definition, into any theory. It is interesting that adherents of the nature
theory seize the regression toward the mean to criticize surveys which are
related to the effect of compensation programs while they, in essence, take
the same statistical phenomenon as evidence to justify their theory[6]. Here
we come to the third variant.

Regression Over Different Groups

Eysenck and Jensen[7] maintain that the genetically expected correlation
between parent and child is approximately .50 and they say that this value
was observed repeatedly. Figure 5 demonstrated, in a formalized manner, how
in that case the relation is between the IQ of parent and child, based on
homogenous groups of parents with a score of 130, 120 etc.

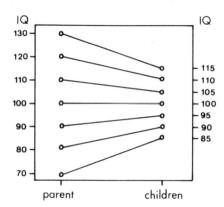

Figure 5   Relation between the IQ of parents and their children, based on a
           correlation r_{xy} = .50.

The parents with an IQ of 100 have children with the same average. Intelligent parents, however, have on the average dumber children, and stupid
parents have offspring who score higher, on average, than themselves. Given
equal means and variances, the amount of regression can be calculated simply. In this example, the distance to the mean decreases by 50%. The authors
see this as an indication of the inheritance of intelligence differences.
The argumentation is twofold. In the first instance, the reasoning is turned around by saying that it is very difficult to explain why it is that
children of intelligent parents, despite proper schooling and a suitable
upbringing score lower, and vice versa. The nurture theory should, therefore, not tally. This assumption is actually quite weak because an adherent
of that standpoint could say that children of intelligent parents spend a
great deal of their time in a less endowed environment (school, neighbourhood, club), with results in proportion. For the time being, this effect
has, however, nothing to do with any theory because we must go a step
further.

The figure can create the impression that intelligence differences are
obliterated after a number of generations, or rather that everyone comes to
100. Figure 6 shows what happens, according to Eysenck.

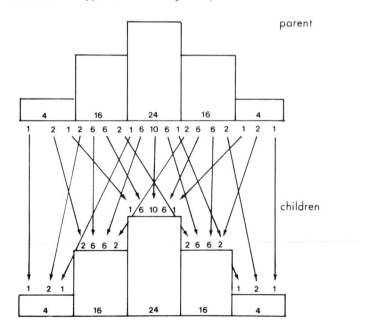

Figure 6   Redistribution of IQ according to Eysenck.

For the sake of convenience, the distributions are drawn in histograms.
Children of moderately intelligent parents become symmetrically spread over
all IQ classes (egression from the mean). Some of the children of parents
who score low, actually end up in the higher classes (regression toward the
mean), and vice versa. Therefore, the IQ is redistributed but mean and
variance remain the same and history repeats itself (the children also bear
children, etc.). Eysenck does not allow any misunderstanding about the
interpretation of this picture. He says that coincidental gene splitting
and new gene combinations are responsible for these effects, and that this
is exactly what would be expected on the basis of genetics. Eysenck means
that intelligence is so-called polygenetically determined, or rather that
"intelligence genes" exist. In this context, amounts between 22 and 100
genes are mentioned in the literature. The effects of these genes are small,
equal, independent, and additive. Analogous to the example of airplane landings, it can be said that they can exceed or fall short of one's expectations. The gene make-up of an individual can, therefore, be compared with a
number of coins which are tossed on a table. It will often occur that the
number of heads is approximately the same as the number of tails (these are
the moderately intelligent people), but in a single case the frequency of
tails could greatly exceed the number of heads, and vice versa. The result
is a normal distribution. In principle, according to Eysenck, the same
occurs with very intelligent or very stupid people. These chances are
relatively small, which provides the basis for the tails of the distribution.

It is clear that such an explanation *can* be appropriate in explaining
the distribution of IQ. Eysenck sees the regression toward the mean as a
genetic mechanism which provides for the redistribution of intelligence.
Since IQ, according to him, lies at the base of schooling, income, and
occupation, a phenomenon such as social mobility also should be explained
genetically. Eysenck takes up the standpoint that no social system can
compete with the graciousness of genetic laws which make sure that no caste
system originates whereby parent and child would stay in the same class
(compare figure 6). Eysenck clearly conceives regression toward the mean as
a force of nature. He says that it almost looks as if we are being sharply
watched by a god who is determined to reduce the differences in IQ which
exist today between various occupations and classes. On the other side of
the coin he remarks that to see your children return to mediocrity and not
being able to do anything about it, thanks to the simple laws of heredity,
is one of the tragedies of life. As a motto for his book, Eysenck says that

hopefully his children will not become victims of genetic regression.
Reasonings with the same tendency are also supported in The Netherlands[8].
Jensen agrees with this. He notes that the correlation between parent and
child in the case of height, is approximately .50 and demonstrates regression toward the mean. Height is, according to Jensen, hereditarily determined;
we find the same phenomenon with intelligence so that this factor will also
lie in the genes. Sir Cyril Burt also took this view and drastically
demonstrated this. Burt[9] states that he tested 40,000 parent-child pairs.
He found two identical distributions. According to him, the correlation
between the IQ of parent and child is theoretically .50, from which 50%
regression results, also regarding social mobility (see earlier). Burt's
data show that this does indeed occur. The problem, however, is that no one
actually ever saw him testing, while he must have had many subjects for
decades. Moreover, the data fit so exactly in his theory that Dorfman
estimates the probability that this was found empirically as one to a half-
trillion. His conclusion is therefore: "The eminent Briton is shown, beyond
reasonable doubt, to have fabricated data on IQ and social class", with
which we come to the unpleasant discussion about the conscious or unconscious deceit which certain adherents of the nature theory would have
committed[10].

The genetic interpretation of regression toward the mean is self-
evidently not the only possibility. An adherent of the environmental theory
could say that the discussed phenomena come from small, equal, independent,
and additive upbringing variables, on the grounds of which precisely the
same can be described and "explained". Humphreys[11] says it clearly:
"Regression is a statistical phenomenon. Biological regression is only one
possible explanation." It can also be formulated another way. Regression
toward the mean does not plead in itself for a single theory. This is
because regression and correlation are closely related to each other and
correlations do not speak for themselves. Only when a theory has been
developed on solid grounds can it be contemplated as including these effects.

Back therefore to statistics. Assume that the correlation between the
IQ of parent and child is indeed .50. The relation between the intelligence
of a large group of parents and children is shown in figure 7. The
regression line of y on x is traced (for the second regression line[12] see
figure 2) which, based on the IQ of parents, reflects the "best bet"
regarding the score of the children. Parents with an IQ of 100 have
children with an equal average who, nonetheless, spread out over various

IQ children

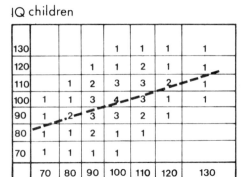

Figure 7   Relation between the IQ of parents and their children, given a
           correlation of .50.

classes (compare figure 6). In regards to parents with an IQ of 70, an
average of 85 is expected for the children (thus, 15 points "profit"), and
vice versa, the offspring of parents with an IQ of 130 average show a "loss"
of 15 points. Figure 6 can, therefore, be found back in this table: there is
egression from, as well as regression to the mean. It is clear that these
phenomena arise because the concerned correlation is imperfect (and because
a straight line is used as a predictor). As means and variances are equal,
the regression comes to 50%. Also this variant of regression, therefore,
reflects nothing else than the imperfectness of the correlation.

In an article[13] Eysenck creates the impression that he is beginning to
have his doubts. After having described his polygenetic model once again, he
says: "It is sometimes suggested that the phenomenon (i.e. figure 6) is
merely a statistical artifact, due to statistical regression produced by the
observed correlation between parents and children. This is not an explanation
because it takes for given some of the things that require explanation, such
as the maintenance, from generation to generation, of equal IQ variances, or
the existence of marked social mobility." This is a very strange way of
reasoning. The test is cooked in such a way that distribution is *created*
and mean and variance are, per definition, constant. Moreover, regarding
social mobility, we at first know little more than that there are
correlations which have to do with statistical regression too (also compare
chapter 3)[14].

Predictions

Correlations do not plead for a certain theory, nor does regression toward the mean. But to do justice to the genetic model, it is useful to express a few expectations with which the data will have to agree[15]. The latter will be discussed in chapter 6.

With identical distributions, i.e. equal mean and variance, and a correlation between parent and child of .50, a simple genetic model says that there must be 50% regression from parent to child[16]. It is assumed then that the parents get married according to chance, or rather that no assortative mating (AM) occured. It is meant here that sometimes a connection is found between the qualities of partners. The correlation regarding heights seems to be approximately .40, which is understandable because it could be seen as a hindrance to have a life partner who is a meter longer or shorter. There is no AM with factors such as eye and hair colour, but for intelligence it is estimated at .40 to .50. This is likely because many contacts are made in the educational and occupational sphere.

The second case contains that people do marry according to chance (random mating), but that the *average* IQ of the parents (so-called mid-parent value) is known. The theoretical correlation with the children is then: $r_{xy}(s_x) + r_{xy}(s_y)/(s_x^2 + s_y^2)^{\frac{1}{2}} = .71$, therefore a higher value. The question is whether, in this case, regression toward the mean occurs. A linear regression line can be written as $y = ax \pm b$. The regression toward the mean is equal to $(1 - a)$. It now applies: $y = r_{xy}(s_y/s_x)x + b$. The variance of the mid-parent value is one-half of the variance of the single parent. Thus, this means that (taking the square root) $s_x = 0.71s_y$. From this it follows: $y = 0.71(s_y/0.71s_y)x + b$, or $y = x + b$. In other words: there is *no* regression toward the mean if we start from the average of the parents and no assortative mating.

Case three regards the assumption, which will likely not meet with objection, that there is AM. In the absence of AM, it can be expected that one-half of the variance of the children is related to the variance of the parents, and the rest is coincidence. The correlation with father and mother must therefore be .50; both contribute 25% of the variance so that we come to 50%. With the average parent, the correlation must amount to .71, which comes to 50% variance when squared. AM makes sure that all correlations theoretically become higher; with "perfect" AM the correlation becomes 1 and, therefore, there is no regression toward the mean. If AM =

= .50 and the mid-parent is the base, then the correlation with the children is equal to $r_{xy}(s_x) + r_{xy}(s_y)/(s_x^2 + s_y^2 + 2r_{xy}s_xs_y)^{\frac{1}{2}} = 0.58$, and regression toward the mean should be observed.

Conclusion

When an object is repeatedly measured, a distribution is revealed. On purely statistical grounds, many distributions demonstrate regression toward the mean. The same occurs if imperfect correlations are dealt with, either in test-retest situations or in comparing different groups. Because regression results from chance, the phenomenon does not plead for any theory and says nothing about mysterious forces which are ascribed by some to genetics.

Footnotes, Chapter 4

1. For a formal discussion see Coleman (1968), Visser (1978)
2. Tversky and Kahneman (1974)
3. Hopkins (1969)
4. Campbell and Erlebacher (1975)
5. Stanley (1967), Molenaar and Tomas (1978)
6. See, for example, the discussion between De Groot and Van Peet on the one hand, and Peschar on the other hand, in the Tijdschrift voor Onder-wijsresearch, 1975.
7. Eysenck (1973), Jensen (1972). De Leeuw (1979) has calculated on which (mathematical) presuppositions Galton's and Eysenck's interpretation of regression toward the mean must have been based. His conclusion is that these authors assume that all women have an equal IQ. Eysenck's book "The Inequality of Man" ought to have been called, according to De Leeuw, "The Inequality of Men".
8. De Groot and Van Peet (1974)
9. In: Dorfman (1978)
10. See also chapter 6.
11. Humphreys (1978)
12. This relates to the regression child-parent and is excluded here as it is not of importance for our goal. The same applies to the variances which the correlations bring along with them. See Humphreys (1978) and McAskie and Clarke (1976).
13. Eysenck (1977)
14. See an enlightening article (Furby, 1973) about this which also covers social mobility.
15. Humphreys (1978) and McAskie and Clarke (1976)
16. See Wright (1921) for calculations on the basis of a simple genetic model.

5 ENTRY OF THE THEORIES

The question asking what intelligence is can be answered in various ways, depending on the scientific philosophy adhered to and the definition level which is chosen. Although, on the grounds of the discussed material, some doubt can arise about the question whether the tests relate anything of importance, the IQ debate already rages on for a century. Central is the issue: to which mechanisms, sources, and variables the observed score differences can be ascribed. For that purpose a division in behaviour is made which cannot be simpler, namely nature versus nurture. The most well-known striving parties use this division. A third trend is represented by, among others, geneticists who maintain that we can speak only in terms of an interplay between heredity and environment. Within psychology there is one social interaction theory (chapter 7). In the course of time, others have concerned themselves with the problem, such as astronomers, physicists, and mathematicians. Their standpoint can be summarized as follows: either the question is meaningless, or the available material does not have sufficient quality to be able to justly draw conclusions.

It could be felt that psychologists, being reasonable people, would be open to each other's standpoints. Remarkably enough, this is hardly the case regarding the intelligence question. The differences in opinion today are approximately the same as those of a century ago. Apparently the parties do no *want* to be convinced, and that can have something to do with political ideas which have been connected of old to the issue. Where principles are mentioned, the power of the argument becomes defunct. The debate is difficult to follow in so far that scientific-philosophical, content psycholigical, methodological, as well as statistical aspects are subjects of discussion. We shall first attempt to raise the issues in general terms, to thereafter inspect the material further.

The Debate

Especially the adherents of the nature theory complain that their
insights have not become common knowledge, while it should be crystal-clear
that intelligence and other properties have their roots in the genes. At
the time[1] Pearson stated: "It is strange that there should still remain any
doubt that psychical characters are inherited at the same rate as physical
characters." With this he remained in the line of the work and the presuppositions of Galton. Ever since then nothing has changed. Hirsch[2]
complains about the great incomprehension concerning the geneticists
amongst psychologists: "The historians of science show that, in fact, very
few people are ever converted from one point of view to a radically new
one", whereby he makes a prelude to the conflict of paradigms in science
(Kuhn, Lakatos, and others). Eysenck feels that the test-retest
unreliability of IQ tests may not be seen as a fact that makes the
calculation of the hereditary component uncertain, but that people who fill
in tests unreliably suffer from hereditarily determined personality factors
which compel them to such behaviour. Therefore, Eysenck is convinced that
he is right and goes so far as to explain away or ignore data which do not
fit in. In The Netherlands De Groot[3] expresses the serious conjecture that
boys, children from higher milieus, whites, and Jews are more intelligent
than, respectively, girls, children from lower classes, negroes, and many
other races, and that little can be done about this because of the extreme
hereditary determination of the differences. Regarding these spectacular
propositions, the reader is not burdened with arguments. De Groot feels
that this is hardly necessary and maybe even senseless, because opposition
rests on prejudices. "Those who are prejudiced are opposed, consciously or
unconsciously, but in any case affectively to alternate possibilities.
Affective resistance against changes belong to the constitutional characteristics of prejudice. Exactly because of this, prejudice is so difficult to
overcome; "'contrary evidence' is usually insufficient". De Groot is
absolutely right. We may note here that defenders of other standpoints have
a reason to state the same. If an environmental theory threatens to the
right, the nature model attempts to challenge publications based, for
example, on statistical regression toward the mean, and they subsequently
bring that same regression in the limelight as an argument for their own
theory.

Under the influence of Darwin's work, the nature theories of the

previous century established the image of differential psychology in general.
Biologists and doctors have frequently adhered to this standpoint, and maybe not lastly because their profession involves attention aimed at processes *in* the organism and not so much at its environment. The phenomenologist
Van den Berg[4] can hardly suppress his repugnance against environmental
theories. Ultimately, the evil force is democracy which has declared everyone to be equal. As a result of this, there are mentally deficient people
because there are schools for the mentally deficient, criminals are made
felonious, and psychotics, he sighs, are so-called not diseased but are
people who are maltreated and shunned by those who are healthy. Naturally,
intelligence is also hereditarily determined, something which doctors in
general claim to know[5]. The environmental theory is, on the contrary,
derived somewhat more from contemporary thinking in the social sciences and
lays the emphasis on environmental variables and (potentially) on the
fundamental equality of man. As we have seen, also this idea is not at all
new, no more than the politically tinged views which are related to that.

Self-Involvement

A platitude says that science is man-made. Self-involvement means that
the strict observation of phenomena is determined by the presuppositions,
norms, and values of the researcher. The degree to which these play a role
will vary with the object which is being aimed at. It is improbable that an
astronomer who shows an interest in the nature of pulsars will allow his
spectral analyses to be coloured by the party he votes for. In psychology
this is different, and due to the fact that the object and subject of
research coincide to a large extent. A researcher of perception is controlled by the laws he attempts to find. Further, the significance of various
psychological concepts is linked to things which the psychologist considers
to be important for himself and others. Like a Rorschach picture can be
interpreted in many ways (per definition), so can "solid" data also be
expressed in more than one way.

Sherwood et al.[6] looked at biographical data from a number of researchers who had been occupied with the study about intelligence differences
between white and black populations. The conclusions about the degree to
which the scores differed and especially about the origin of these
differences, were rather divergent. The psychologists who stemmed from the
lower classes and whose family members had not resided very long in the

United States, were inclined to come across a smaller difference than the
"real Americans" from higher circles, and they preferably interpreted these
in terms of divergent milieus of whites and blacks. The correlation between
the biographies and the nature of the conclusions reached the value of .55.
Pastore[7] reports that from twelve researchers who defended the genetic
standpoint, eleven belonged to the conservative party, and that almost all
defenders of the environmental theory considered themselves to be liberal
left-wing. Eysenck[8] discounts such studies with the remark that those
involved, after learning the "facts", then chose their political attitudes,
but that does not explain the cohesion of their ideas with origin and life
course. Moreover, Eysenck does not know at what point the political choice
was made.

A second and annoying side of the debate is the deceit that is said to
have been practised by various researchers. What we sometimes forget to
report when making such a judgment is that experiments were formerly often
only used to illustrate the scope of ideas with some numbers. Under the
influence of positivism and physicalism, many psychologists chose the
reversed path, where the past appears in a new light.

The most sensational case is that of Sir Cyril Burt who did important
work for the nature theory[9]. Burt worked together with two mysterious ladies
who sometimes appeared as co-authors (Howard and Conway), but who could not
be located after the death of Burt in 1971. Burt, Howard, and Conway have,
among other things, written a fair number of book reviews. Their styles were
extremely similar so that some suspect that the ladies were pseudonyms of
Burt. If this is true then Burt had an imaginative mind, because in his
articles he sometimes thanks them or he states that certain work (tests, for
example) were performed by Howard and Conway. Burt's estate consisted of six
tea crates of papers which were vaguely inspected by Hudson and were
unfortunately thrown away. Because of this much figure work cannot be judged
anymore. There is, in any case, something remarkable about his studies on
monozygotic and dizygotic (MZ and DZ) twins. With 21 separately raised pairs
Burt reports in 1955 a correlation between their IQ scores of .771 and that
same figure was later found accurately to the third decimal with more than
30 and with 53 pairs (1966). With MZ twins who were raised together, the
correlation is .944. A possibility is that Burt calculated the correlations
once and assumed that this would also apply for different amounts. Looking
at the statistical work performed by Burt, this assumption is actually very
naive. Then there is a problem that Burt does talk about tests and testing,

but says little or nothing about the nature of them or the procedure used.
Further, scores are sometimes "finally assessed" but no one knows exactly
what that means. Finally, there is an issue that Dorfman pays attention to
and that was discussed earlier, namely the fabulous precision with which
40,000 parent-child data fit into Burt's theory (see chapter 4). Apart from
that, the adversary Kamin is reproached in turn[10] that he handled numbers
carelessly and suggestively, Lewontin[11] raises the same point in relation to
the tables of Jensen, and also Layzer[12] makes a contribution in this case.
Therefore, there are in relation to the data itself quite some problems of
a diverse nature. Similar discussions add little to the image of psychology.
To soften this it can be said that the natural sciences have also known
scandals of this nature[13].

Genetics and the Nature Theory

There are many biological, psycholigical, social, cultural, income,
national, and international differences between people. Various sciences
attempt to consider these whereby mixing all the differneces does not
clarify anything in advance, or claiming that one type of difference is
responsible for all the others. Many physiological and perhaps also psychological phenomena and possibilities do not come from nowhere but have to do
with heredity[14].

Man develops from an egg and a sperm cell which each contain 23 chromosomes. In mating, the number of possible chromosome combinations is 2^{23}. The
number of chromosomes does not increase with the complexity of the organism;
a potato, for example, has more than man. In fact, the (developmental)
processes are established by the genes. It is estimated that each chromosome
has about 1300. This means that there are $2^{30,000}$ possible gene combinations
through which an enormous variation can be genetically expected. With this
it can also be considered that the total number of people who have lived so
far does not come to more than 10^{11}. Spatially seen, genes do not mean much.
The DNA which lies within the genes has the volume of half an aspirin for
all mankind. Hereditary characteristics are carried over through the inter-
change of the genes from the mother and father (crossing over). After one
fused cell comes into existence 44 divisions follow after which the child is
born, and after another 4 divisions the stage of adulthood is reached. The
genes lie in pairs (alleles) at fixed points adjacent in the chromosome.
There is no mingling of the genes at the time of impregnation, but the

alleles divide and join. In principle this means that genes have an
individuality and maintain it, and that many characteristics are controlled
by pairs of genes, originating from father and mother. This division rule is
the first law of Mendel. A few decades ago it was discovered that one gene
can influence the properties of other genes. It has not been proven, however,
that this occurs because of direct influence from the surroundings (against
Lamarck, therefore).

A second principle is the dominance law which says that one gene can
check the influence of another (dominant versus recessive). When we call A
the dominant gene and a the recessive gene regarding a certain quality there
are, therefore, three combinations, AA, Aa, and aa. If the colour of a
flower is established by one gene then AA can be a red flower, aa a white
one, and Aa is then pink. There are in this case only three genotypes. If
the colour, on the contrary, has something to do with two genes (A and B)
there are nine possibilities: AABB, AaBB, aaBB, AABb, aaBb, AAbb, AaBb,
Aabb, and aabb, or rather many more colour variations. Pairing recessive
genes contains that the respective property will be less pronounced.

Everyone has mutated genes which do not promote the development of
certain properties. Mostly these genes are recessive. If a child is produced
according to chance then the probability of a combination of two mutated
genes which have to do with the same property is very small. This
probability increases, however, in relation to the genetic proximity of the
partners (in-breeding). If the family is healthy then usually nothing
happens. In antiquity in-breeding was very common to keep certain things in
the family. Marriages between brother and sister often occurred in Egypt
(which was not always without problems, however), and in the Bible before
the time of Moses it was customary to marry family members. Abraham married
his half-sister Sara (Genesis 20) and the mother of Moses was the sister of
his grandfather on his father's side (Exodus 6). This was stopped by Moses.
The Roman Catholic church later adopted this. An exception is still made in
some farming villages where the money of families is collected through
fitting marriages. The in-breeding phenomenon is also known in the
laboratories where it often occurs that rat colonies are decimated as a
result of this. Pairing recessive genes can, in any case, bring problems
along with it. Charles Darwin married his niece Emma Wedgwood. Three of
their ten children died young in spite of the fact that they were properly
cared for and one was mentally handicapped.

It is clear that this simple presentation of facts can lead to the assumption that dominant and recessive intelligence genes exist (see chapter 4) which each would have a small, equal, independent, and additive influence on IQ. That some actually believe this and, moreover, are of the opinion that these genes are differently distributed over races, appears in the following quotation from Jensen: "The number of intelligence genes seems lower, overall, in the black population than in the white."[15] Others go somewhat further and say that the Y chromosome, the male thus, is responsible for the higher performance in spatial insight which is shown by IQ tests taken by men[16].

Finally, the independence law is known which says that uncorrelated properties can exist (the eyes of the father, the hair of the mother, etc.). These three laws are known as Mendel's laws (1822-1884). An example of the independence law is the offspring of a white and a negro. In regards to the skin colour, the eyes, the hair, etc. these mulattoes are a mixture of their parents, which was a reason in the past to speak of a "blood mixture" rather than of the mixture of (more or less discrete) properties. The descendants of mulattoes, however, demonstrate considerable variation, that is, some children look very much like negroes, some like whites, and others more like a mixture. With mulattoes the "negroid" and "white" genes are divided arbitrarily over the genital cells, but they seem to maintain their independence.

Genes can become damaged and mutated by various influences. Certain forms of radiation are an example. Heat, however, also seems to be dangerous. Montagu contends that the scrotum of a naked man is on the average $3.3^{o}C$ colder than someone who is wearing trousers, and the effect of the latter on the occurrence of mutations could be compared, looking at a whole life span, with the damaging influence of a quarter of a million x-rays of the chest. Therefore, back to nature.

There are hereditary deviations which can be related to intelligence, among other things[17]. Approximately 40 innate metabolistic diseases are known which can lead to a low IQ, but innate is not the same as hereditarily determined. In most of the cases the genetic basis of the disease is unknown. In some cases there is something that is known. One chromosome (number 1 and 18, for example) may appear three times (trisomy). If that occurs with chromosome 21 then mongoloid idiocy is encountered[18]. Other suspected genetic defects which, amongst others, cause a defective development of intelligence are the syndromes of Klinefelter and Turner. According to Richter and Engel, it applies however that a genetic defect is found with not more than 10% of the feeble-minded.

Montagu emphasizes that we must not speak of genes operating in isolation but that there is always a cooperation with the environment. Others follow him in this. Geneticists are undoubtedly right but on a psychological level this remark is not very interesting because the concept "environment" is hardly defined. It seems to come down to *all* influences that reach man from the first cell division, and that amount is undetermined. Nevertheless, there are examples which are clarifying. The metabolistic disease PKU (phenylketonuria) has to do with one gene which is capable of unsettling the whole body, including intelligence. The disorder is, however, not irrevocable provided it is discovered at an early stage. If the children receive a diet for one or two years then nothing will happen. In a diagram this comes down to the following:

		environment (diet)	type
		1	2
PKU gene	yes	normal	disturbed
	no	normal	normal

Only the combination of the PKU gene and diet 2 leads to problems whereby the question is rightfully asked where the "cause" lies. The disturbances only occur given *both* a genetic disposition as well as certain environmental influences. The importance of this interaction is also pointed out by Bodmer who says that the nature of PKU demonstrates another important point; the expression of a gene is strongly influenced by the environment. PKU individuals show a substantial variation. This indicates that the genetic difference which is related to PKU is by no means the only or even the most important factor. In other words: a genetic defect can, according to the nature of the environment, be paired with considerable variation of the phenotype (the ultimate result) and further, some genes appear to be able to influence a large amount of others, which is not totally in agreement with the mentioned polygenetic model (the equal, small, independent, and additive influences on intelligence).

The work of Fisher from 1918 takes a central position in the nature theory. Fisher used Mendel's theory as a base and argued, on the grounds of different grades of genetic affinity, which relations should be disclosed regarding various characteristics. His article is extraordinarily difficult to read which has led to a number of exegetic publications that far exceed the size of the piece. In a certain sense Fisher has therefore written the

Finnegans Wake of biometric genetics. In any case, Burt, Jensen, and others base themselves on this model. In essence, it is about an agrarian issue, that is, the crossing of plants. In that framework, the environment is a disturbing factor which can be manipulated well (temperature, moisture, fertilizer, etc.). In this case it is possible to describe the environmental factor and to influence it. With people that is considerably more difficult for the simple reason that we scarcely know what intelligence is and, consequently, also cannot put a finger on the precise environmental and upbringing factors which have to do with that. The nature theory regarding this is very simple. It is certain that intelligence is innate and the search for environmental determinants is, therefore, not extensive. As a result of this uncorrelated occupational classes, for example, also mean uncorrelated environments, but we know nothing about that. It is quite conceivable that the relevant environmental factors cannot at all be ascribed to factors such as family income and the status of the father, viewed from a certain social perspective and value pattern.

The work of Fisher is continued in the form of so-called biometric population genetics. This means that collections of creatures are chosen such as caddis flies, bed bugs, stickleback, and people and, given the environmental variation, an attempt is made to calculate how much of the phenotypic variance could rest on genetic factors. De Leeuw[19] is not particularly exuberant about this. He says that population genetics assume that both heredity as well as environment are properly defined and measurable factors. This is certainly not the case with man so that little could be claimed. The fact that something is called genetic does not mean that it *is* genetic. An example is height. It is claimed that the phenotypic variance can be ascribed approximately 90% to hereditary factors but the geneticist is not certain what to do with the fact that the average height of man has increased considerably over the last three generations. The same has been mentioned regarding the IQ test: between the two World Wars the IQ of recruits increased one whole standard deviation, and also that can hardly rest on genetic processes.

The Standpoint of the Nature Theory

It is useful to give a summary of what the nature theory precisely says[20].

1. Man is much more nature than culture, which means that he is relatively

insensitive to changes in, and influences from society in the broadest
sense of the word, from upbringing thus, up to and including schooling.
The IQ test measures intelligence and that concept refers to a general,
innate, and stable property. Therefore, they want nothing to do with, for
example, multi-factor theories which unnecessarily complicate the issue.
Intelligence is *g*. According to Burt, intelligence does exist. Tests are
insufficient instruments, the results of which can and must be adjusted
by making estimates[21].

2. IQ forms the basis of success at school and in the occupational sector.
   Also, social mobility is mainly determined genetically.

3. Biometric genetics has to do with populations. This means that the
   descendance factor of a quality is not fixed for everything and everyone.
   With the white population it applies that approximately 80% of the
   phenotypic variance is hereditary. Herrnstein combines 2. and 3. in the
   following syllogism: "If differences in mental abilities are inherited
   and if success requires those abilities, and if earnings and prestige
   depend on success, then, social standing will be based to some extent on
   inherited differences among people."

4. Differences between races and social classes are (sometimes) large and
   are presumably blamed on the gene package. The nature theory (mainly
   expressed by Herrnstein) links a social theory to this. Social mobility
   is and *must* also be established by IQ, and wealth will (supposedly) be
   acquired by the intelligent. Society benefits from the fact that they
   constitute the rules. IQ and reward are and must be highly correlated
   (the so-called meritocracy, whereby the social merit of someone apparently has everything to do with his IQ). In connection to automation, IQ
   and education are becoming more important. This means that stupid people
   are threatened with becoming unemployed, and this is annoying because
   "the tendency to be unemployed may run in the genes of a family as
   certainly as the IQ does now", which appears to mean a new (Lamarckian)
   genetic law. A government that strives for equality and unchecked social
   mobility brings itself, says Herrnstein, and society in great difficulty.
   The expulsion of heavy and tedious labour means misery for the unintelligent who can do nothing else, with pauperizing as a result. That can be
   avoided by not changing the social order.

5. IQ demonstrates strong resistance against attempts at change. Aspiring to
   (more) equality of races and classes, for example, using compensation
   programs rests on utopistic "leftist" fantasies. De Groot and Van Peet

talk about unattainable egalitarian goals.

That nature theory, social Darwinism, and eugenics are still related, appears in some quotations from Jensen's work. "There are intelligence genes, which are found in populations in different proportions somewhat like the distribution of blood types.... The techniques for raising intelligence per se, in the sense of g, probably lie more in the province of biological sciences than in psychology and education."

The Environmental Theory

The antipole of the nature model is the environmental theory which proceeds from the premise that all are created equal (compare chapter 1) and that differences in terms of IQ, income, occupation, and status are a matter of (not) receiving opportunities and a proper upbringing. In this framework the question is also asked if man is preeminently nature or culture. The latter means that environmental influences, norms, and values are the most important for development. These factors can be ascribed to various types of entities. One type consists of biological variables about which Hoorweg has written a dissertation[22].

He studied a number of Ugandian children with an average age of 14 years. Given a measure for the social environment, IQ correlated negatively with a medical index for chronic undernourishment. The deterioration was the strongest with spatial reasoning and spatial insight. If factors were concerned such as rote learning, memory, and language then there was no or only a very low correlation, which seems to be an indication of a multi-factor theory of intelligence. What can be the explanation? A low weight at birth could lead to those children having more trouble from undernourishment than others. This does not appear to be true because the correlations had nothing to do with weight at birth. Further, a large study in The Netherlands carried out on 20,000 men who (with an average low weight at birth) were born during the famine winter (1944), and whose average IQ later (on the basis of the Raven Progressive Matrices) appeared to be normal. The second possibility is that the discovered effect is of a genetic nature, in that sense that stupid children suffer more from undernourishment. Hoorweg found no indications for this when he also looked at the IQ of the parents. The third possibility appears to be fairly realistic. An undernourished child also lives in a limited stimulating environment in other ways. Mother has more things to do than to devise intellectual games. Undernourishment and

little attention can lead to passivity from the child so that the mother
stimulates the child even less, resulting in a vicious circle. In any case,
the undernourishment must last a long time and be very severe to produce
effects. A physiological hypotesis contains that during the first years of
life in the brain, millions of links between the nerve cells develop for
which both stimulation as well as proper nourishment are essential[23].

Interesting is the general issue: to what degree is man considered to
be a creature of nature? This question is difficult to answer because no one
seems to know what the antipole, culture, exactly means. In any case, a
number of tall tales are known about *homo ferus*, the wild man[24], this in
opposition to erectus, sapiens, ludens, and so on. Approximately 20 cases
are known of children who ended up (from an early age or somewhat later) in
some way, in an environment which is not seen as pedagogically justified. At
the end of the 18th century the wild boy of Aveyron was encountered in the
forest. At that time the boy was about twelve years old; he was naked, and
lived on acorns and roots. He did not speak but growled and ran like an
animal. His communication consisted mainly of biting and scratching. His
sense of pain was not very developed because he took potatoes out of a pan
of boiling water with ease. A gunshot scarcely frightened him away but he
turned himself around like lightning if a walnut was cracked in the vicinity.
After five years he could still not speak, and his learning achievements
were much lower that what had been hoped. Another example concerns two girls
who were found by a missionary in India around 1920. He found them in the
company of a wolf. They were captured and walked on all fours. At night they
became active and stalked, howling like wolves. They slept curled up
together on the ground, showed a dislike for people, chose a rotten chicken
rather than a well-prepared meal, had a very sharp sense of hearing, and
could smell meat from great distances. One of the girls died soon. The
other never learned to walk and after six years her vocabulary consisted of
only 40 words. A more recent story is about a girl, Anna, who was locked in
a room for a very long time. In spite of loving care the same type of
phenomenon occurred, that is, the social contact and the intellectual
development proceeded laboriously and slowly.

The tendency which is connected to such anecdotes is that pedagogy is
a very important subject and that man can best be described as an *animal
educandum* which hardly has a nature, but is formed excessively by the
environment. Along with this the renowned concept "critical period" arises
which, in connection with animal tests, is seen as a phase where certain

processes *must* be established. If that does not happen then the damage is great and will be difficult to make up for. With adults this is known in the form of the congenital blind who later, via an operation (often cataract extraction), could see. Some never learned to handle the new stimuli chaos and therefore put on welding glasses[25].

In a review by Clark[26] the problem of the effect of early experience on the development of man is discussed. A number of reports and also experiments are seriously criticized, among other things on the grounds of the recommendation that those involved apparently had not realized precisely *which* upbringing measures should have been taken. As a result of that, the conclusion about the barely reversible effects should sometimes not be correct whereby the arrows are also pointed at Harlow and his too well-known and unethical tests with the monkeys that were rendered pathetic. Further, it is said about the wild man that some rather unreliable information has been put in print and that it is not inconceivable that some wildmen were autistic, that is, children who also under "normal" circumstances would have grown up to be rather deviant people[27].

Conflict is the father of all things

This remark by Heraclitus sketches a too rosey image of the nature-nurture controversy in so far that the war has led to nothing[28]. It is a misunderstanding to suppose that people are convinced by arguments and numbers. What is an argument for one is not for the other, and a number and a fact are not the same. Nature versus nurture is, according to Overton, a "paradigm clash", that is, a conflict between presuppositions which is difficult to change. He feels that none of the parties in connection to the vagueness of concepts such as heredity and environment, really know what they are precisely talking about, by which the whole debate is little more than a number conflict, the raising of opportune arguments, and not in the last place, selective quoting from the literature. It can be added that the trends swear by research techniques, heuristics, and preferences which are difficult to combine.

A few examples. If an adherent of the genetic theory observes that a certain IQ test shows results other than what was predicted, it is attributed to the fact that the test is good for nothing in the sense that this does not sufficiently bring the factor *g* to light, the test was not properly taken, the subjects were improperly instructed, or the test was not culture-

and education-free. In connection with g the last is considered very important; one of the twins on Nova Zembla must manifest the same as his brother
or sister in Springfield. In opposition to the nature model, the environmental theory is mainly in search of tests that demonstrate the equality of man,
given identical milieus. If this is not correct then it is also caused by
the instrument of measure, of course, in which framework Lewontin[29] remarks
that 13 tests are used in combination and thrown on one pile which makes us
think of an attempt to establish the quality of a soccer team by calculating
the average of their shirt numbers. This messing around with tests is
possible thanks to the operational definition of intelligence, and it is to
be expected, therefore, that such polemics will keep on being published for
a while.

If a compensation program is not successful then that is evidence for
the nature theory. The environmental model usually excuses itself with
remarks along the lines that the study was improperly executed or that the
right moment was not chosen, as well as again criticism regarding the test.
In general, it applies after all that the theories construct tests which
agree the best with the ideas in advance. With the nature theory g is
strived for (hence the resistance to the Guilford model); the environmental
theory grasps for everything which appears to offer results.

Urbach also gives a sketch of the controversy in an article that is
otherwise rather biased in favour of the nature idea. He says that a strong
point of the environmental theory is that it is based on the equality of
classes and races, while the nature model can say nothing about this.
Against this, the last provided predictions in terms of correlations about
the relation between the IQ of people, given divergent genetic relations.
The environmental theory objects that higher correlations which would go
together with closer genetic relation also imply higher correlating milieus.
Urbach finds that insipid because the environmental theory does not name any
figures and the nature model does. This remark is not fair in so far that
the genetic model contains remarkable simplifications so that also the
environmental theory might present some numbers on a similar basis. On the
contrary, the environmental theory is weak in that, for example, it tries to
explain away the high correlations between the IQ of MZ twins in different
milieus by saying that the milieus do differ but that it cannot be shown in
what way and to what degree. Taken strictly, however, this could again
concern the nature theory which also does not know if environments can indeed
be taken as uncorrelated. For this the factors in the milieu must be known

which have to do with intellectual growth.

Urbach is in the wrong with his proposition that the redistribution of father on son was found so well by Burt and fits in the genetic model with the 50% regression toward the mean. The first is not true because Burt probably made up his material in this respect, and the second rests on statistical regression which, as such, makes a plea for nothing.

The environmental theory (again) says, about the differ ces between classes, that the test is no good, that the upbringing does not concur, but further explanations are not given. The discussions about the wellknown adoption study of Skodak and Skeels[30] are also interesting. They found, given an average IQ of biological mothers of 85.5 that their children in foster homes had an average IQ of 106. According to the genetic model that should not be true; the regression toward the mean predicts 93, given that the fathers reached a score of 100 (see chapter 4). The justification is that the biological fathers had been considerably more intelligent. However, nothing is known about that. Other objections are that the children were probably specially selected, and even that the IQ of the biological mothers, because of the stress near the day of the birth, came out much too low, an excuse that is never thought of if an adoption study does agree with the "genetic" predictions.

Still another aspect concerns the differences between races. On certain IQ tests whites score higher than Indians and these are again somewhat better than negroes. The environmental theory is not sure what to say about this. The average Indian is in a miserable position, and what about the intelligent Eskimo's who live under very primitive circumstances? The "explanation" is then that the growing up in an igloo brings along good, stimulating family ties, which Urbach (justifiably) discounts as "empty verbal quibble". For the rest it must be added that also the nature theory has no explanation for race differences, other than in terms of pronouncements about the intelligence genes, but that is a tautology. The environmental theory also ascribes many differences to the test attitude of the negro. He would feel inferior in relation to a white psychologist with deplorable results, etc. In discussions of the gigantic program Head Start, which according to some has had little success, the adherents of the environmental theory go quite far when they propose that mysterious forces have caused the whole to fail because otherwise social reforms should have been necessary, which the government did not want.

The interaction theory has been omitted up to now. The reason for this is that it is woven into the nature theory. It is time to glance at the data.

Footnotes, Chapter 5

1. Pearson (1918)
2. Hirsch (1967)
3. De Groot (1970)
4. Van den Berg (1964, 1970)
5. Jonkees and Vandenbroucke (1975)
6. Sherwood and Nataupsky (1968)
7. Pastore (1949)
8. Eysenck (1973)
9. Kamin (1974), Jensen (1974), Dorfman (1978), Wade (1976), Jaspars (1976)
10. Fulker (1975)
11. Lewontin (1975)
12. Layzer (1975)
13. See for example Koestler (1971)
14. See for example Montagu (1959), Novitski (1977)
15. Jensen (1972, 1978)
16. Huttenlocher, in: Resnick (1976)
17. Ritter and Engel (1976), Bodmer, in: Montagu (1975), Montagu (1959), Kempthorne (1978)
18. It is called this because it was felt earlier that these children remained at the level of the mongoloid race (Montagu, 1959)
19. De Leeuw (1977)
20. See for example Daniels (1976), Herrnstein (1971, 1973), De Groot and Van Peet (1974), Eysenck (1973), Jensen (1972, 1978), Colman (1972)
21. Eysenck (1978) claims that approximately the same applies for homophily (to be seen from the form of the pelvis), neuroticism, various personality characteristics, and criminality.
22. Hoorweg (1976)
23. Here it is felt that much is known on the grounds of animal tests which can be left out for our purpose.
24. See Schmidt (1973), Linschoten (1964)
25. Some of this can be found in the classical and, according to some, dubious publications by Von Senden.
26. Clarke and Clarke (1976)
27. See Vroon (1978) for (speculations about) autistic patients.

28. Urbach (1974), Overton (1973), Kaye (1976)
29. Lewontin (1975)
30. Skodak and Skeels (1949)

Differential psychology is concerned with the seeking out of individual differences and with contemplations about the origin of them[1]. Natural abilities are not directly observable so that procedures must be sought to reveal them. An old idea holds that certain bodily characteristics (skull, lower jaw) are chosen as a point of departure for the estimation of intelligence[2]. Further, height is highly regarded in this area, a factor which is normally distributed and, according to Burt[3], is hereditarily determined for 94.3% of the variance.

Here analogical reasoning is used: biological properties are often normally distributed and genetically given; therefore, the same will likely apply to intelligence. Criticism is apparent. The distribution of intelligence is unknown; genetics does not know for sure at all whether, or to what degree, height lies established in the genes[4], and it is not very easy to explain that the average height of man seems to have increased 2 standard deviations (12 cm.) in the last century. A possibility is that nutrition and education substantially change a population characteristic. The latter could also apply to intelligence. The method used to understand the heredity of intelligence rests on statistical compilations of various data such as adoption, twins, correlations between parents and children, in-breeding phenomena, etc.

The nature theory naturally has a reluctance against multi-factor theories. The human cognitive ability is genetically determined and thus is stable and general. Nuances do occur however. Burt feels that intelligence can be measured very well with tests, and Herrnstein also approves of this. The tests are, however, faulty instruments of measure which can be improved by the researcher in partly estimating scores whereby the real intellect becomes manifest. As a result of this, the highest heredity coefficients can be found with Burt. Jensen is more careful in this respect. He utilizes an operational definition of intelligence and does not agree that the numbers

are changed by estimation. Therefore, Jensen has repeatedly disqualified
Burt somewhat[5]. De Groot[6], on the contrary, names the various guesses
"scientific" and poses that Burt always worked very carefully.

The Heredity of IQ

The work of Burt et al. has become of interest again when Jensen wrote
a long article in 1969 entitled *How can we Boost IQ and Scholastic Achievement*. In the first sentence of that article he says that compensation
programs were applied on a large scale and had failed. Jensen scarcely looks
at the why of that eventual failing but uses (his interpretation of) the
available data to provide an explanation in the form of IQ as hereditarily
determined. There came about 200 predominantly angry reactions against the
article but Jensen was certain of his case and stated that he was not at all
impressed. The basic equation of his theory[7] is a linear and additive model:
$V_p = V_g + V_{de} + V_{am} + V_e + CV_{ge} + V_i + V_{er}$. V_p is the variance of intelligence such as that encountered within the population (the phenotype). The
extent of this is per definition 15^2 or 16^2 thus 225 or 256 (depending on
the choice made for the size of the standard deviation). The total variance
is decomposed into a number of sources. This occurs by analysis of variance
which is a general term for a large number of methods[8]. In principle, the
same applies here as for factor analysis: so-called sources of variance can
be found statistically, but the *name* of it will not be provided by any
computer. Thus, this means once again that a factor is not bound to heredity
or environment because that word is chosen.

V_g is the additive variance which is genetically determined. This has
to do with the similarities between parents and children. Were V_g the only
factor, then the intelligence of children would correlate .50 with that of
their parents.

V_{de} has to do with dominance and epistasy. Theoretically the 22 to 100
IQ genes[9] have two forms, namely dominant and recessive (compare the coin
model in chapter 4). Although no one knows if such intelligence genes exist
it provides no obstacle for the nature model to come to suppositions and
package them in a separate variance component. If the intelligence of the
heterozygote Aa lies between AA and aa there is no dominance. If A and B are
different intelligence genes, epistasy makes sure that their combined
influence is greater or smaller than the sum of the individual differences.

V_{am} is related to assortative mating. Between parents no correlation exists regarding fingerprints and colour of eyes, but with height a value of approximately .35 can be observed and with intelligence this would be about .40 to .50. The effect of AM is presumably that the variance of the population increases. In other words: through AM the differences between children within different families are less than those between children of different families. Because of the increasing variance the tails of the IQ distribution become filled. Since people with a very low IQ propagate less (idiots, imbeciles, etc.) it is presumed that the net effect of AM over a number of generations works as an intelligence-increaser. Jensen feels that without AM the number of talented people (IQ higher than 130) would become more than halved in time and the number of very talented people (IQ from 145) would diminish all the way to one-sixth. Therefore, in a certain way AM has (unintentional) eugenic effects.

V_e is the variance which has to do with environmental influences. The assessment of this is not simple because it must be known which environmental factors are important. In practice a measure is often chosen which is based on income. Thus, it is assumed that cognitive development and money have much to do with one another. In finding a milieu index in practice a large number of problems are attached, because we still do not know what intelligence is, and consequently we have just as little insight into the question which asks what precisely must be viewed as important in the environment. Does a cubic meter of toys provide a stimulating influence? Or is it essential to have a bookcase full of philosophy? Do sisters continuously playing the spinet have a beneficial influence? Due to the lack of theory the estimation of the environmental variance is consequently a case which rather rests on the fantasy of the researcher.

CV_{ge} is the so-called covariance of nature and environment. This means that there is a correlation between the natural ability of the child and the environment in which he grows up. No one knows how large this is (so that we are forced to estimate), but the idea is that genetically advantaged or disadvantaged children grow up in a milieu which adapts to their talents. This can be imagined by saying that a child partly creates his own environment. An intelligent child asks for an encyclopedia during his toddler years; a dumb child desires only nursery rhymes for Christmas. Because correlations say nothing about causes, this term can be attributed to both the hereditary and to the milieu factor. Inasmuch as this could be disputed here, various interpretations exist.

V_i has to do with the interaction of nature and environment, or rather

the given that different genotypes react differenctly to the same surroundings. It can be conceived that an imbecilic child will not benefit from a
balanced elementary school program but that an intelligent child under
similar circumstances blossoms. Some tests have been done in this area with
selective breeding of dumb and smart rats whereby IQ is defined by the
speed with which the animal can make its way through a maze. With dumb rats
a "normal" upbringing and a situation of deprivation makes little difference.
There is, however, a large difference if they are raised in normal or in an
extra stimulating environment. With the intelligent rat, on the contrary,
especially the distinction between normal conditions and deprivation is the
determining factor. Another example is that people with the same weight and
activity level react differently to the same food. One becomes fat and the
other does not. If it is now agreed that obesity is a genetic issue, then
it also applies for the interaction term. Also, the effect of diets on the
disease PKU can be considered as interaction.

Finally, V_{er} is the variance coming from the test error. Eysenck is so
enthusiastic that he declares (see earlier) that this term must also be
partly interpreted genetically because the unreliable filling-in of tests is
also an issue that is hereditarily determined.

The heredity coefficient h^2 is calculated by dividing the hereditary
factors (usually everything except V_e) by V_p - V_{er}. Burt's[10] calculations
are interesting. He comes to an h^2 of .82 based on data from children whereby the test agreed with the opinion that the teacher had about the intelligence of his pupils. In this case the covariance was 10.6%. With a number
of children the scores were corrected if the test outcome did not concur
with the opinion of the teacher. The factor h^2 now became .92, the covariance was reduced to almost nil, the test error became (naturally) smaller, and the genetic variance increased. On the grounds of this we may
therefore fear that calculating is a somewhat uncertain happening.

The nature theory bases itself on a number of phenomena. The study
about MZ and DZ twins occupies a central position. MZ twins are considered
to be genetically identical. Thus, when they are separated (shortly) after
birth and grow up in divergent milieus, a comparison of the correlations
between their IQ scores with those of MZ twins raised together provides an
estimation of h^2. Moreover, the MZ twins must reveal higher correlations
between their IQ scores than DZ twins who are genetically as much or as
little related as other children within the same family. The nature theory
makes predictions about the correlations between the intelligence of persons

who vary in the degree of genetic relationship. The examples chosen according to chance must show a correlation of nil, with nephews and nieces the expectation is .25, for parent versus child and the mutual correlation of the children .50 applies, and the MZ twins will have to approach the correlation 1 if they are raised together. Some data[11] show that the correlations do indeed become higher when the ladder of hereditary relationships is climbed, whereby it can be noted that perhaps also the milieus, whatever is understood here, become more homogenous. Data from Burt agree the best with the predictions; according to him, the correlation between parent and child is .492 whereby AM would be .40.[12] Two other points of view are adoption and a lowered IQ as a result of in-breeding. Finally, the regression toward the mean, discussed previously, plays an important role[13].

The predicted correlations are linked to the "law of incestral inheritance" by Galton. He presupposed, in connection with his theory and eugenic program, that in one way or another all forefathers were represented in the individual. If r is the correlation between parent and child, then r^2 is the value for grandparent versus grandchild, r^3 applies to great-grandparent and great-grandchild, and so on. If it is assumed that all forefathers are in the child r *must* be equal to .50. The series $r + r^2 + r^3 + \ldots = r/(1 - r)$ only becomes 1 if r + .50. That Galton just steps over from correlations to proportions of variance will be disregarded as the law is sophistry.

Two Methods

The nature theory uses two calculation methods, namely analysis of variance and path analysis. From the first point of view, h^2 is usually estimated to be .80, which therefore means that 80% of the phenotypic variance is attributed to hereditarily determined factors. Within this technique a large number of models are known which can be chosen.

Broadhurst et al.[14] do not believe that there is covariance and explain that phenotype and genotype as well as environment are normally distributed. The first is, per definition, correct because of the way in which the tests are constructed, the second is an assumption, and the third will amaze as we do not know what environment means. Others in this field [15] hardly encounter an interaction between genotype and environment. Their explanation of this has a circular character: the tests which are used have a large genetic component so that environment is of little importance. It is clear that this is exactly what must be proven.

Another method is path analysis (see further) which is applied by Jensen and especially by Jencks[16]. Proceeding from a correlation of .50 between the IQ of parent and child he reaches, including the covariance, an h^2 of .48 while the environment would take up 52% of the variance. Jencks points out that a high h^2 says nothing about the possibilities of change. The disease PKU has an h^2 of about 1 but as we have seen the effects of the disease can be easily prevented by a simple act from the environment (diet). Jencks' conclusion about the heredity of intelligence is otherwise rather negative: "Indeed, our main conclusion after some years of work on this problem is that mathematical estimates of heritability tell us almost nothing about anything important."

The Issue of Calculation

There exist a number of serious misunderstandings about h^2 and how to calculate it that requires clarification. In the first place, h^2 is a factor describing a population, which means that nothing can be said about an individual.

In the second place, (a high) h^2 in no way means that the quality in question is stable, that is, impervious to external interventions.

In the third place, h^2 is not a constant such as Π or the Avogadro number but a ratio. The more variance is attributed to the environment, the smaller h^2 is. Theoretically h^2 is nil in a caste society based on India's model with very unequal opportunities, and is one in a classless society where everyone is said to receive the same opportunities. This brings us to an interesting paradox: the politically Right Wing tinted nature theory is right if a Maoistic society or something similar is strived towards; the Left Wing environmental theory should actually strive towards unprecedented discrimination.

A fourth misunderstanding is very widely spread. Assume that h^2 is equal to .80 and that the environmental variance is .20; what is then the ratio nature to environment? Andriessen et al.[17] and many others say 4:1. Eysenck[18] takes the square root of this ratio and therefore comes to 2:1. However, the issue is much more complicated[19]. If h^2 is equal to .80 it applies that 90% of the variance in terms of standard deviation is attributed to hereditary factors. However, to be able to say something about the ratio of nature versus environment the correlation between the genotype and the environment must be known, pure nature therefore and the milieu. The standard deviations of phenotype, genotype, and environmental variance can be conceived of as the sides of a triangle. The correlation in question is the negative cosine of the angle between the standard deviation of genotype and environment. The ratio in question is strongly related to the size of this angle A. Assume that s_g is the standard deviation of the genotype, s_e that of the environment, and s_p the standard deviation of the phenotype. It now applies that $s_p^2 = s_e^2 + s_g^2 - 2s_e s_g \cos A$, or rather $s_e^2 + s_g^2 - 2s_e s_g r_{xy}$ where r_{xy} is the correlation to be estimated between genotype and environment. Assume further that $h^2 = .80$, therefore $s_g^2 = 0.8s_p^2$, or rather $s_g = 0.9s_p$. It now applies: $s_e = -r\, s_g + \{(r^2 - 1)s_g^2 + s_p^2\}^{\frac{1}{2}}$. This means that the ratio $s_e/s_g = \dfrac{-0.9r + (0.8r^2 + 0.2)^{\frac{1}{2}}}{0.9}$. If $r = 0$ the ratio nature to environment is 2:1, if $r = 1$ we find 9:1, and with $r = .20$ it is 3:1. If $h^2 = .50$ (Jencks) then the extreme values are 1:1 and 2.3:1. It is clear that the first ratios will change in favour of the environment if $h^2 = .20$. Therefore, given h^2 nothing can be said about the ratio in question because we must know an unknown correlation. Another point is the question whether h^2 is indeed as constantly .80 as the nature theory claims. Jaspars[20] names .12 and .95 as extremes found in the literature. Kamin ends up at nil and says: "There exists no data which should lead a prudent man to accept the hypothesis that IQ test scores are in any degree inheritable."[21] The h^2 of various tests, social classes, and races[22] would lie between .03 and .72. There are also differences between countries. In general, h^2 is lower in the United States than in England. This can have something to do with divergent calculation methods and with (the estimation of) the size of the environmental variance. In general, it applies that h^2 is partly a reflection of a certain culture and a certain educational system[23]. Andriessen et al.[24] remark in this case that h^2 has increased in many countries after the introduction of compulsory education. The environmental variance has decreased so that an increase of h^2 resulted.

The situation becomes even more confusing if the multi-factor theories are looked at[25]. With seven factors h^2 lies between nil and .75. There are also differences between the sexes[26]. With girls h^2 would be .67 for language and with boys only .27. For mathematics almost the reverse applies and h^2 with school performance lies, strangely enough, much below that of intelligence[27]. Adults have a lower value[28], namely .12 as opposed to .75.

As was mentioned, there are two calculation methods, namely analysis of variance and path analysis. De Leeuw[29] employed the first method.

According to him, it applies that a number of studies with twins and
resemblances between children who are brought up separately or raised
together can be calculated statistically in as many as 126 different ways,
whereby h^2 lies somewhere between .20 and 1. He holds the view that finding
a source of variance still does not say anything about its name. Lacking a
theory about the how and the why, genetic differences between brothers and
sisters can also be described as variance resulting from different treatment
based on different external features. As a conclusion he states the following: "The fact that some gene-environment models, based on unrealistic and
usually even silly assumptions, fit the data well, does not mean anything.
If a model that is unrealistic fits the data well, then the data must be
unrealistic. If a silly model fits the data well, then the data must be
silly. If somebody believes a silly model, then that somebody must be
silly."

A second technique for interpreting correlation is path analysis which
is used by Jensen as well as Jencks. An explanatory example follows. Assume
that we want to know what influence visual attention of the mother has on
the IQ of the child. The first is operationalized as the time that the
mother looks at the child divided by the time that they spend together in
the same space. Measurement of both variables occurs at two points in time,
t_1 and t_2. The number of possible causal relations is depicted in figure 8.

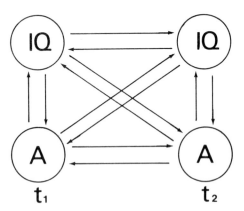

Figure 8   Possible causal relations between IQ and attention (A) by
          measuring at two points in time, t_1 and t_2

The causal influence of the one on the other is expressed by a path
coefficient which can lie between 0 and 1. In the example there are 12

possible paths. They cannot all be calculated because there are maximally
six correlations available (indicated by the double arrows). Therefore, a
number of theoretically possible paths will have to be eliminated. We lose
four paths by assuming that occurrences in the future have no influence on
the past so that there are eight pats left, which is still too many. We
further assume that at t_1 and t_2 there is no immediate influence of A on IQ
and the other way round, whereby we again lose four paths. Ultimately, four
paths remain. Two of these indicate the stability of IQ and attention (A),
the remainder has to do with the influence of one variable on the other. We
must, therefore, come up with four causal relations. The problem now is
that IQ and attention at t_1 do not come from nowhere but that they do have
a history. This beginning correlation (B) stands outside the system as
depicted in figure 8 and its size will have to be estimated. Further, one
can hardly assume that IQ and A at t_2 are only influenced by these same
variables at t_1, but that other factors are also involved. These are indicated as the variables C and D and they may also be correlated (double
arrow). This is depicted in figure 9.

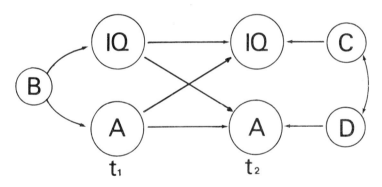

Figure 9   Imaginary path analysis model of the relation between attention
           and IQ

Given an estimate of B, C, and D as well as the correlation between C
and D, the four paths which make up the system in a stricter sense can be
calculated in terms of a path coefficient[30]. The moral is clear: in
principle it is possible to translate correlations into causal relations
but to arrive at a model a number of things must be assumed. Divergent
estimates lead to different results.
     In regards to intelligence, Jensen and Jencks[31] employed this

technique. The path model of Jensen for twins is summarized as follows:
$h^2 + e^2 + 2r + m^2 = 1$, $h^2 + bo^2 + 2r = c$, and $gh^2 + bo^2 + 2r = c^1$, where it
applies that:

c = the observed correlation between the IQ of MZ twins,

c^1 = the observed correlation between the IQ of DZ twins,

h^2 = the ratio of genetic and total variance,

e^2 = the ratio of the environmental variance and the total variance,

m^2 = the unreliability of the test, therefore the ratio of the variance of
     error and the total variance,

g = the genetic correlation between DZ twins,

b = the environmental correlation of MZ twins, and

r = the correlation between genotype and environment.

Numbers can be found in the literature about the values of c and c^1 which
are rather divergent, but from which Jensen makes a choice. The size of b
is not precisely known because the fact that MZ twins grow up in a certain
environment does not mean that they are treated the same. Therefore, Jensen
estimates this value. The factor g must also be estimated; on the grounds
of a genetic model .50 is usually chosen. Also e^2, m^2, and r have to be
mainly filled in on the grounds of guesswork. Given the estimates in
question, Jensen finds a value of .80 for h^2. Other researchers have other
preferences, so that on the grounds of the same data concerning c and c^1
they have come to an h^2 between .15 and .72, which differs about a factor 5.
The calculation of h^2 is therefore very susceptible to changes in estimated
parameters.

Jencks had to endure much in this context[32]. The author recommends his
book as "the best effort at describing the determinants of adult success in
America". He names an h^2 of approximately .50 but says that the value can
easily lie between .25 and .65. The model is not at all a closed one; 78%
of the income variance remains unexplained (so that luck appears to have
more to do with income than, for example, intelligence) and education and
income also hardly have anything in common. Besides this there are various
problems with the calculations. If x has an influence on y, a path
coefficient can only be calculated if y has no influence on x (recursion
principle). Jencks attempted to bypass this by omitting many variables.
Moreover, the measurements must be at least placed on an interval scale and
it is very questionable whether that applies for IQ and occupational
prestige, which Jencks has included in his model. The variables must also
be additive, whereby Jencks does not mention the many possible interactions.

Finally, he also estimates some factors such as the genotype of the child (which is naturally a rough guess because each test can only be taken when effects of the environment are already established), and the correlation between the family's IQ and the family's education. If other values are filled in the path coefficients and h^2 point in all directions. Another point is that Jencks partly bases himself on old studies of MZ and DZ twins, whereby it cannot or hardly cannot be traced whether it was really about MZ or DZ twins. Taylor's conclusion is therefore rather angry: "All things considered the Jencks volume really cannot be taken seriously."

Twins

Research with DZ and MZ twins still occupies a central position. According to the law of Hellin, on the average one pair of twins is born per 87 births. Multiple births are powers of 87, triplets therefore occur one time per 87^2 births, etc.[33] MZ twins develop from one egg, are of the same sex, and are considered to be genetically identical. According to Montagu[34] this applies to approximately 25% of twins. In the case of early separation a very diverse life course can often be seen. Montagu reports, for example, that in only one case out of 18 both children committed suicide. MZ and DZ twins are traditionally distinguished by comparing them on a number of criteria such as external resemblance and/or a simple blood test. There are no other possibilities because no one was watching while the cell split. The criteria are not fixed, they are a question of choice. For example, one researcher only wants to speak about MZ twins if the fingerprints are the same, the other focuses on eye and hair colour, equal height, etc. Thus, this means that the identification of MZ twins is partly a matter of discretion. Furthermore, twins who are called MZ on the grounds of similar external characteristics can have different antigenes in their blood[35]. This raises a not insubstantial problem. If we agree that a certain collection of twins are of the MZ type and, for example, their antigenes are different then the statement "genetically identical" is surrounded with uncertainty. With intelligence we do not know *which* (genetic) characteristics are of importance so that it is very well possible that the distinctions made in the literature are hardly relevant. Concretely, this holds that the research of twins that is highly regarded is really not so easy and obvious. In other words: the chances of confusing MZ and DZ regarding that which is important for IQ are unknown.

First some figures[36]. According to Eysenck, the correlation between the IQ of MZ twins who are raised together is approximately .90 and with a separate upbringing, approximately .80. The slight decline is naturally an argument for the genetic determination of intelligence. If intelligence is totally hereditary the correlation in both cases would be 1. Munsinger says that the number with MZ twins who are brought up together lies between .76 and .94; with DZ twins it varies from .44 to .66. Jensen notes that there are only four studies about separately raised MZ twins with a total of 122 pairs. The correlations lie, according to him, between .69 and .86 with an average of .81. Others report a correlation of .77 over 37 pairs (we will omit the very high and miraculously constant correlations of Burt). Jensen feels that the correlation can directly be taken as h^2; various research-ers[37] are, however, of the opinion that this is incorrect and the result is an overestimation of h^2. Jencks comes to an h^2 of .50 also based on twins.

There are various problems in this area. A strange phenomenon which various authors[38] point to is that multiple births score lower on the average which cannot be explained genetically. Jensen thinks that this must be ascribed to the less pleasant circumstances in the womb. Eysenck[39] reports that a doctor in South Africa has attempted to influence the IQ of the unborn child in a positive way by, every now and then, creating a vacuum in the womb of the mother. The blood circulation of the womb would thereby be improved. However, an effect on IQ has not been observed.

A difficulty is at what age the MZ twins are separated and how different the milieus are wherein they are accommodated. For example, using occupation-al classes (Burt) it can be postulated that the environments are un-correlated but this statement assumes a *theory* about environment and intel-ligence which is lacking. Also, it often occurs that the children are not separated immediately after the birth but not till a while later. We do not know how far the basis for their intellectual development was already established at that moment[40].

Another point of discussion is the so-called selective placement. This means that adoption agencies do not work according to chance but attempt to place the children in comparable milieus[41]. Husén feels that this has occurred often and that Jensen's h^2 of .80 should be replaced by .50 (which is also a gamble because Husén does not know what is understood by milieu either). Selective placement means that the environmental variance becomes relatively slight causing h^2 to come out high. In practice it is pretended that the milieus do not correlate so that the differences in correlation

between the IQ of separated and collective upbringing would directly refer
to the hereditary component. With correlating milieus the slight decline of
the correlation of MZ twins can, however, be ascribed to comparable treatment. Newman et al. note further that in one study the separated MZ children
differed from the control group who stayed together. The age of the separated
children varied at the time of the study between 11 and 59 years, which
brings test problems along with it, and as a division criterium the factor
"temperament" was employed, among others, with the result that we, according to the authors, do not know how accurate the divisions of the groups
was. There is also an age problem in the Juel-Nielsen study and the fact
that the environments were perhaps not uncorrelated. Moreover, conclusions
are drawn here on the grounds of only 12 pairs. Shields says that many of
the separated twins had mutual contact and that they were often brought up
in different households within the same family, so that it would be difficult
to speak of uncorrelated milieus.

Still another problem is that according to some, MZ and DZ twins live
in the same environment physically but not psychologically[42]. Scarr found
that with 61 female pairs of twins the parents would have made a mistake in
the question whether they were DZ or MZ twins. It appeared that some pairs
were treated more equally than others and that the external characteristics
was the criterium here. MZ twins would therefore, regarding their IQ (also)
correlate highly because they look so much alike and are equally treated,
dressed, etc. Also Lytton found that MZ twins were treated more equally than
DZ twins. According to him, the behaviour of the parents would however rest
on the nature of the child, and not on the perception of it. If an MZ twin
is seen by accident as DZ the parents behave in the same way as with an MZ
twin. If this is true then the different correlations with MZ and DZ twins
can therefore not be completely ascribed to the environments.

Smith also disputes that the milieu for MZ and DZ would be the same.
According to him MZ children are treated fairly identically. In 262 pairs
the parents made a mistake with 13.5% of the MZ children which were seen as
DZ; with the DZ twins the error percentage was 28. According to Smith, some
of the equality of MZ children is definitely caused by the behaviour of the
parents. MZ twins had the same friends, eating habits, the same clothing,
domestic pursuits, personal preferences, and a basically identical self-
image, this in opposition to DZ children. All of this would again mean that,
in general terms, the milieu of MZ and DZ twins is not the same. Kamin has
the same opinion and asks himself whether the similarity is genetically

determined or not. An interpretation in terms of environmental influences would hold that MZ twins look more alike than DZ, and DZ twins more than brothers and sisters in the same family who are born after each other. Genetically there should be no difference between DZ twins and other children. According to Kamin, the correlations between the IQ of DZ twins is mostly *higher*, which therefore supports his hypothesis.

These and similar difficulties are summarized in a study by Adams et al. in the thesis that, on the grounds of the study of twins, (still) nothing can be said about the hereditary determination of IQ.

Correlations Between Parent and Child

The nature theory predicts that the correlation between single parent and child must be .50, whereby we exclude selective partner choice. Burt[43] names a value of 0.492 which does agree well, but other sources demonstrate some dispersion. Jencks reports values between .35 and .58. Tyler mentions a gigantic spread, namely from .20 to .80, and adds that often very different tests are used for parents and children and that there are very few relevant data. In connection to the problem of measuring intelligence, it is important that the test data from the parents originate from *their* childhood years and that is rarely the case. Moreover, parent and child actually ought to be studied using the same test.

Erlenmeyer-Kimling and Jarvik refer to the same point and claim the record with a spread between -.73 and +.70. Important in this context is a review article by McAskie and Clarke[44]. The genetic model says that half of the variance of the children is attributed to the parents; the rest is coincidence. This means that the correlation between the father and the child and the mother and the child must each be .50, which gives 25% + 25% = 50% variance. It is assumed here that there is random mating. The correlation between the mid-parent and child to reach the 50% variance must therefore be .71. Assortative mating increases the theoretical correlations[45]. If AM is equal to .40 the correlation between single parent and child must be equal to .50 plus half of AM, and thus come to .70. The correlation from the mid-parent must, in this case, be 1. Regression toward the mean naturally does not appear. As we have seen in chapter 4, this also applies to the correlation with the mid-parent of .71. If the correlation with the single parent is .50, the regression is theoretically 50%. With attention to the upbringing it can be assumed further that the correlation between mother and daughter, and that between father and son is perhaps somewhat higher than with the other combinations.

In short, the findings of McAskie and Clarke are as follows. Empirically the parent-child correlation lies between a negative number and .80, which naturally does not simplify testing. There are no differences in the domain of father versus son, mother versus daughter, and such. Indications of dominance of the highest IQ (of mother or father) were also not encountered. The correlations with the children are somewhat lower in the (rare) cases that the parent was tested as a child and with very intelligent parents there were scarcely any correlations with the children.

On the average, correlations are lower than are expected on the grounds of the genetic model. The correlation with the mid-parent is not .71 but lies between .35 and .70. The regression toward the mean from the single parent varies strongly but is on the average (indeed) 50%, which agrees very nicely if we interpret the phenomenon purely statistically (see chapter 4). The mid-parent should not demonstrate regression; this is however averaged at 39%. The conclusion of the authors is self-evident: regarding the relation of parents and children the nature model is not correct.

Adoption and In-breeding

Now the studies about adoption. The rationale here is that children are separated from their biological parents and are brought up elsewhere. The influence of heredity would be established by comparing the correlation of .50 with the biological parent mentioned earlier, to the correlation with the foster parents. A problem here is again that the correlations behave like buckshot: in 55 studies [46] about the correlations between children who were raised together a variation between .30 and .80 was found. Jencks reports that non-genetically related children who are raised together reach a correlation of .38 which would point to a not insubstantial influence from the environment. Further, it is important not to stop at the observation that the correlation of children with their foster mothers, for example, is lower than that with their biological parents, but that it is also tested whether the difference is *significant*. The latter is omitted rather often[47]. Lewontin[48] mentions a study whereby the first correlation was .39 and the second was .35. This naturally does not mean that intelligence is mainly determined by the environment, because the difference

means nothing statistically. Kamin says that the correlation between
adoptive parents with their own children would be .35 and with the foster
children .26, which (in this case) is not a significant difference either.

The study of Skodak and Skeels[49] is still renowned. They
observed that the correlation of adopted children with the IQ of their
biological mothers was .44, but that the correlation with the foster mother
was around nil. This suggests that IQ is mainly genetically determined but
there are hidden dangers here. The average IQ of the foster children was at
a certain moment 106; that of their biological mothers was only 85.5. Assume
that the biological fathers (of whom we know nothing) had an average IQ of
100, then the genetic model predicts that the IQ of the children should
have been 93 which still lies 13 points below the observed value. Another
point is that strict selective placement would have occurred often[50] and,
in this sense, that the most intelligent children were relegated to the
"best" milieus. In the third place it applied that the variance of the IQ
of the foster mothers was much smaller than that of the biological mothers
with the result that the probability of finding a significant correlation
strongly decreases. Lastly, Kamin reports that the correlation between the
educational level of the biological mothers with the IQ of their to-be-
adopted daughters was .44 and was nil with the boys. Genetically this cannot
occur.

This brings us to general methodological pitfalls which are related to
this type of research. It often applies that parents who adopt have a high
social status and have none or few children of their own. Because of the
relatively slight variance in their IQ finding of correlations with foster
children is improbable[51].

Munsinger[52] wrote a review article on this subject. He commences by
arranging the studies with the aid of methodological criteria. A few of
these are as follows. Adopted children would not form a random sample from
the population insofar that their parents are often more than normally
intelligent (this did not apply for Skodak and Skeels). Further, selective
placement must be guarded against ("fitting the home to the child"); often
poor and incomparable tests are used, often nothing is known about the
fathers, and the children must go to foster homes at a very early age. The
adoptive parent is often ten years older than the biological mother which,
in connection with education and such, can bring in more differences in
relation to the biological parents which subsequently could appear in the
IQ (unjustly). Finally, in choosing extremely low scoring children

regression toward the mean occurs.

Using similar criteria, Munsinger assessed 17 studies between 1922 and 1975. Only 4 studies could pass the test of his criticism. The work of Skodak and Skeels and that of Freeman et al., which appear to make a plea for an environmental theory, were judged as poor. Munsinger finds that the correlation with the adoptive parents is .20 on the average and says that the correlation with the biological parents is approximately .58. His conclusion is therefore that IQ is mainly hereditarily determined. Kamin[53] retorts that according to Munsinger's criteria, whose own research makes a strong plea for genetic determination, (naturally) is methodologically set up the best, and that for example the work of Freeman et al. which aims at the opposite is no good. Kamin blames that on the fact that Munsinger incorrectly describes Freeman's study and in such a way that he denounces it by using his methodological criteria. Munsinger's reply reads in summary that data can, however, be looked at and calculated in more than one way, whereby we again return to the "swamp" which was described earlier about the calculations of h^2.

Lastly, something about in-breeding, a phenomenon that via the pairing of recessive genes within the family can lead to many disorders. Eysenck[54] cites a Japanese study from which it would appear that in-breeding goes together with so-called IQ depression, which naturally must be interpreted genetically. The publication of the researchers itself does not justify this conclusion at all. They did indeed encounter both a lower IQ as well as poorer school performance but explain that such a complicated system of relations and influences is involved that no conclusion may be drawn in terms of a genetic mechanism.

Occupation, Income, Classes, and Races

As was mentioned, the nature theory unravels the correlations between IQ, occupation, income, and social class in favour of the IQ that would be the hereditarily determined source of all other differences. A distinct opinion of this can be found with Eysenck and Conway[55], among others. Regarding both IQ as well as social mobility regression toward the mean also stands central, which is interpreted as genetic redistribution and not as a statistical artifact. Herrnstein connects to this an overwhelmingly simple social theory (chapter 5). Andriessen et al.[56] agree with this. They feel that differences between social classes are mainly genetically

determined and quote with agreement the almost exact 50% regression of Burt.
The authors foresee a so-called hereditary meritocracy. Because manual
labour occurs less and less in modern industrialized societies in favour of
mental labour, IQ is becoming more important. According to them, assortative
mating will increase which contributes to a rise of h^2. Socialism may (say
that they) strive for a reduction of differences in terms of income and
education opportunities but because of that the environmental variation
becomes smaller and h^2 therefore higher (it is about ratios). The authors
forget to report here that more equality could theoretically also lead to a
smaller spread of intelligence scores, and in that context h^2 is not important at all. If little differences would remain it is hardly interesting to
know whether these are hereditarily connected or not. In any case, a merito-
cratic caste system is awaiting us, where the top group with the high IQ's
have the power.

The authors mention three possibilities to be able to do something
about this. The first is "genetic engineering", that is, tampering with
genes or rather a modern variant of the earlier eugenics; "social engineering", that is, attempts to change intelligence scores, for example, by
setting up special improper schools and increase low IQ's; and finally,
leaving the connection between education and income.

De Groot and Van Peet[57] concur with this in a broad sense. It is
strange that they always talk about a *certain* degree of the hereditary
determination of IQ. All numbers between .01 and .99 correspond with this
which does not stop them from defending the hereditary view with its
implications. Presumably nothing can be expected from compensation programs;
differences between social classes (and races) are for the greater part
genetically determined and the regression toward the mean is also seen by
them as an important argument in favour of the nature theory. In accordance
with the biblical parable about the talents, the authors contend that the
value of a person is determined by what he has done with his natural
ability. However, this is not so easy to measure in a pure form and therefore also cannot be expressed in money (income). Attempts to introduce more
equality in society rest on egalitarian utopias[58].

Gray[59] goes somewhat further still. He assumes that h^2 is approximately
.80 which would mean that 80% of the *absolute* difference (therefore not the
variance) would be hereditarily linked. Gray feels further that the distribution of IQ has remained the same over the last 50 years which is used as
an argument for its stable, genetic foundation. Gray is right, provided that

it is mentioned again that the distribution, per definition, does not change
as long as we construct tests in the usual ways and come to agreements about
the distribution of scores. Moreover, he says that Burt's observations
clarify that IQ is an important determinant for the question asking to which
societal class one belongs, and that intelligence naturally also has everything to do with unequal incomes. The question can again be asked here what
Burt actually observed and what correlations have to do with causes. Finally,
also Gray says that social mobility is caused by IQ which in turn is subject
to genetic regression.

A story in itself concerns the background of IQ differences with
various races. For the sake of brevity it can be remarked that the nature
theory also feels that these have a genetic foundation[60]. Statistically this
brings a problem along with it[61]. If differences *within* populations are (may
be) genetically linked, then this says nothing about differences *between*
populations. Assume that we choose a population of professors (A) with an
average IQ of 140 and a group of shrimp-peelers (B) with a value of 80.
Assume that h^2 is equal to .80. Further V_g means the genetically linked
variance and V_e is the environmental variance. The same number of specimens
are chosen from both groups ($p = q = \frac{1}{2}$) and are joined to form one new group.
The variance here is now $pq(A - B)^2 + V_g + V_e$. The first term in this case
is 900 and regards the unnameable between variance. Proportionally seen, V_g
hardly plays a role now.

At the level of content an article in this context has been published
by Furby[62]. Assume that an hereditary factor within populations also says
something about the genetic determination of differences between populations.
Then there are unfortunately five possibilities.
1. A variation in skin colour exists within the population of Dutchmen and
Spaniards. This likely has to do with the degree of exposure to the sun and
is therefore mainly determined by the environment. The between variance,
however, will likely have a genetic component.
2. Assume that height is hereditary within a population but that the amount
of milk consumed also plays a role. The population is divided into two
"environments": considerable and low milk consumption. Two distributions of
height will probably develop (which partly overlap). This means that genetic
determination within groups can go together well with environmental
influences which describe the differences between the groups. In this case
it is clear that, in principle, upbringing and IQ can be used in the place
of milk and height. An agrarian example: two handfuls of wheat are taken

which are grown without self-pollination and consequently show much genetic
variation. One part receives perfectly balanced nutrients; from the soil of
the rest essential elements such as nitrogen and zinc compounds are removed.
The result will be that two populations will develop with a different length.
In both cases $h^2 = 1$ applies for the within variance but the milieu is
totally responsible for the differences between the populations.

3. Assume that half of the variance is hereditary and that the rest is
determined by the environment. Group A drinks, on the average, 1 glass of
milk per day, group B averages 3 glasses. Assume further that "milieu" is
the same as the amount of milk. If a difference occurs between the height of
A and B this is caused by the milk (milieu). Assume further that there are
two groups with different genotypes for height and that they are all exposed
to the same environment, being averaged at 2 glasses of milk per day. It
will now apply for both groups that half of the within variance rests on the
changing milk consumption and the other half on genetic factors. However,
inasmuch as the genotypes differ, the between variance is genetically
determined. This is transferrable to class and race problems; it is very
well possible that both genotype as well as milieu are divergent in regards
to intelligence. If a difference between, for example, white and black is
found we do not know if the genotype is responsible or the environmental
factors. The observed difference can have a hereditary basis, a background
that has to do with milieu, or both. A repeatedly raised argument of the
nature theory is that also relatively rich negroes are, on the average,
dumber than whites and that the difference would consequently be genetic. It
is clear that this conclusion cannot be drawn as such because it is not
known whether *money* is the (milieu) factor. Maybe it has to do with
attention of the mother, domino stones, or an alcoholic father. There are
researchers[63] who, on the grounds of data about black and white twins, came
to the conclusion that the IQ differences can be ascribed to both
environmental variation as well as to interaction between nature and milieu.
Many[64] tried very hard in this context to find a measure for environment,
whereby they consider income, family size, occupation of the father, amount
of stimulation the child receives, the school, etc. A solution is not
provided; the authors are satisfied with the description of 12 possible
research plans to discover this.

4. Still another possibility is that the within variance in one group is
more strongly determined genetically than in the other. We will again choose
milk and height. Assume that in connection with the possible calcium intake

it is of no use to drink more than 2 glasses of milk per day. The one group
drinks 3 glasses on the average (and therefore is above the limit), the
other 1 glass per day. The one group drinks too much and individual differences therefore mainly reflect the genotype, which results in a high h^2.
With the second group the milk is a "true" milieu factor that counts, with
the result that h^2 must come out lower (the environmental variation in the
form of the changing consumption around the average of 1 glass per day is
now responsible for much of the height variation). Therefore, in this case
there are different groups with a different h^2 for height. The within
variance is genetically related, the between variance is caused by the
milieu.

5. Again assume two groups. Group A possesses genes which determine height
and which require milk to be able to utilize their influence. The genes of
group B require gin to reach the same goal. Assume that both groups are
introduced to the same milieu, with the requirement that they all receive a
lot of milk to drink and little gin, with, respectively, high and low
variance. Group A will now become taller than B and h^2 of B will naturally
come out higher (little milieu variation). About the difference between the
averages we can only vaguely say that changing interactions between genes
and milieu exist.

Thus, differences between races and classes can be interpreted in many
ways from which a choice can only be made if more intelligence theory is
available than at the present. Possibilities are genetic differences, interaction, covariance, milieu, limits, etc. In any case, the comparing of
socioeconomic status says nothing as long as we do not know what is important about this status regarding the intellectual development.

Conclusions

It is necessary to be a brave man to declare that it is *clear* that IQ
is genetically determined. It would be incorrect to claim that heredity
plays *no* role but the question here is in what sense this is the case.
Some[65] find that the whole problem is not worth mentioning and there is
something to be said for that. It must at least be known what intelligence
is and what milieu is before a search can be made for the origin of differences. We arrive now at a more or less scientific philosophical level[66].

It can be defended that the crucial experiment has not been performed
yet and for the time being can also not be conceived. Given conceptual

confusion and obscurity, methodological and statistical refinements are of
no use. That psychology does not appear to know precisely what is meant by
heredity is witnessed by the fact that descriptions such as relation,
activity, process, fact, property, material, organization, rule, resemblance,
connection, and contributory influence are used. As we shall see, approximately the same applies to the environment. In any case, inseparable interactions will exist. If it would be decided not to educate people with red
hair or blood group B negative, their IQ will approach the limit nil but
that does not mean that the IQ is (partly) hereditary, like the blood group
and the hair colour.

In The Netherlands illiteracy is caused by a mental defect, or perhaps
blindness. In India the most important cause is lack of educational
possibilities. These hardly play a role for us but in India so much the more.
Further, it applies that the same "objective" environment can be totally
different subjectively for various genotypes, whereby a disease such as PKU
can again be thought of.

Assume finally that an MZ twin demonstrates 10 IQ points difference
with upbringing in divergent families and that there is 30 points difference
with groups of two unrelated children who are brought up within the same
families. Can it now be said that the 10 points is a representation of the
difference between both milieus and that the difference of 30 points may
therefore be divided into 10 for the environment and 20 for heredity? The
answer must be negative because a small genetic difference between the unrelated children can have led to the active "stimulus value" of the milieus
for the children being considerably different. It is hardly useful to talk
about uncorrelated and constant milieus. We do not know what uncorrelated
is, and what is "objectively" constant does not have to be constant for a
child who lives in that milieu.

The more that is thought about the question what nature and milieu
could mean, the stronger they become intertwined, and the stranger it
becomes to think of these as a dualism.

Footnotes, Chapter 6

1. Jaspars (1975, 1977)
2. Jensen (1978), Eysenck (1977, 1978)
3. Burt (1958, 1970, 1971, 1973)
4. Bodmer, in: Montagu (1975), De Leeuw (1977)
5. Jensen (1974, 1978)
6. De Groot (1972), compare also chapter 5
7. For calculation methods see the explanations about the so-called polygenetic model: Burt and Howard (1956), Jinks and Fulker (1970), Burt (1971), Jensen (1972), Eaves (1969), De Leeuw (1977)
8. See Winer (1970)
9. Broadhurst et al. (1974), Jinks and Fulker (1970)
10. Burt and Howard (1956, 1957), Burt (1958)
11. Erlenmeyer-Kimling and Jarvik (1963)
12. Burt (1971)
13. Eysenck (1977) further names biological properties (jaw bone), phenomena which would occur in orphanages that are characterized by a uniform environment, and the so-called "evoked potentials" which can be observed from the electroencephalogram when a subject is sensorially stimulated. See also De Leeuw (1979).
14. Broadhurst et al. (1974)
15. Jinks and Fulker (1970)
16. Jencks (1972)
17. Andriessen et al. (1973)
18. Eysenck (1973)
19. Layzer (1972), see also the weak defence of Jensen (1972) and Herrnstein (1972), as well as Emigh (1977).
20. Jaspars (1977). The highest number (almost 1) can be found by Munsinger (1977).
21. Kamin (1974)
22. Scarr-Salapatek (1971)
23. Husén (1975), Brody and Brody (1976)
24. Andriessen et al. (1973)
25. Vandenberg (1967)
26. Montagu (1975)
27. Jensen (1972)
28. Rao et al. (1974)

29. De Leeuw (1977)
30. Kroonenberg (1979)
31. Jensen (1972), Jencks (1972), Van Tilborg (1977)
32. Taylor (1973)
33. We will not consider the over-representation of multiple births that
    is occurring presently as a result of the use of hormone injections
    made from the urine of pregnant women.
34. Montagu (1959)
35. Compare Haverkorn et al. (1975)
36. Eysenck (1977), Munsinger (1975), Jensen (1972), Jencks (1972), Smith
    (1965), Shields (1962), see Wright (1921) for theoretical calculations.
37. Mills and Levine (1973), Linn (1974), Jensen (1971)
38. Jensen (1972), Zajonc and Markus (1975)
39. Eysenck (1973)
40. Riksen-Walraven (1977)
41. See Husén (1975), Newman et al. (1937), Juel-Nielsen (1965), Shields
    (1962), Loevinger (1943), Scarr and Weinberg (1976)
42. Hogarth (1974), Scarr (1968), Lytton (1977), Smith (1974), Kamin (1974),
    Adams et al. (1976), Freudenthal (1976)
43. Burt (1971), Jencks (1972), Erlenmeyer-Kimling and Jarvik (1963),
    Tyler (1972), Eckland (1976), Newman et al. (1937)
44. McAskie and Clarke (1976), compare also chapter 4
45. Eckland (1967)
46. Erlenmeyer-Kimling and Jarvik (1963), Jencks (1972)
47. Husén (1975), Kamin (1974)
48. Lewontin (1975), Freeman et al. (1928)
49. Skodak and Skeels (1949), see also Honzik (1957)
50. Lewontin (1975)
51. Brody and Brody (1976)
52. Munsinger (1975)
53. Kamin (1978), Munsinger (1978)
54. Eysenck (1973), Schull and Neel (1965)
55. Eysenck (1973), Conway (1958)
56. Andriessen et al. (1973)
57. De Groot and Van Peet (1974)
58. See De Klerk (1979), Vroon (1976) also makes rather senseless remarks
    in this context.
59. Gray (1974)

60. See also De Groot (1970)
61. Compare Milkman (1978) for a rather trivial and unrealistic calculation method using rectangular distributions and numbers chosen randomly.
62. Furby (1973)
63. Scarr-Salapatek (1971)
64. Walberg and Majoribanks (1976)
65. Colman (1972)
66. See Anastasi and Foley (1948)

7 INTERACTION

Another possibility of interpreting differences between IQ scores holds that there is interplay of factors. The literature in that area consists of two types. A motley crowd of experts on psychological, but also physical, astronomical, mathematical, and genetic grounds explain that divisions into dichotomies such as nature versus environment are fruitless for divergent reasons. (The same applies for other seemingly clarifying divisions such as mind-body, person-culture, etc.). The nucleus of their argument approximately holds that the question in that form is unsolvable and not interesting. Apart from this there are some psychological theories which attempt to explain intelligence differences from a mainly micro - social perspective.

The Useless Dichotomy

The psychologist Anastasi[1] demonstrates that all behaviour is a function of nature and environment but that these factors are inseparable. In regards to one or other characteristic, a population has an h^2 which only applies under certain conditions. With intelligence h^2 can be decreased by introducing more environmental variation than what is available at present. However, a simpler trick is to allow the existing environmental variation to weigh heavier. That is hardly interesting because it is not about h^2 but about the *size* of the differences between people and the consequences of this for their education, housing, occupation, and income. Further, one variable may fluctuate as a function of the other, i.e., the environment operates differently on different genotypes. Conversely, a genetic factor can be felt, in a greater or lesser degree, under changing environmental influences. According to her, this can be seen with various races such as black and white in America. If the income is especially related with races (discrimination) and the background of this is the genetically established skin colour, the income (per definition) also has a high h^2.

The statistician, Kempthorne[2], assumes the position that man possesses
and must possess an enormous arsenal of cognitive abilities which, for the
most part, cannot be captured in tests. As an example he mentions the
mathematician and physicist, Poincaré, who continued to remain at a score of
a mental defective regardless of repeated attempts. This remark is insipid
insofar that an instrument should not be cut off because it fails to serve
its purpose once. Kempthorne further aims his remarks at analysis of
variance which does provide sources of differences but which says nothing
about their name and about "causes". Assume that 50% of the IQ variance is
environmentally determined. If the environmental conditions could be
improved by 2 standard deviations, this leads to an IQ profit of $(0.5)^{\frac{1}{2}}$ x
x (2 x 15) = 7.5 points. Assume that group 1 belongs to a low social class
and has an average that lies 7.5 points lower than a higher class 2. The
averages would have to become equal if we provide the first group with a
better environment by 2 standard deviations, which holds that the milieu
would now be in the 95th percentile. Subsequently, the argument can be turned aroud: if it is to be explained why group 1 scores lower it must be
assumed that the group belongs to the 5th environmental percentile. According to him, we know nothing about this due to a lack of a theory about
"environment" and conclude therefore, for convenience' sake, that the
distinction between the groups has a genetic basis. According to Kempthorne,
there is only talk of statistical relations which throw no light on causes,
no more than it is reasonable to explain on the grounds of a correlation
that 80% of the yearly variation of the birth rate is caused by the number
of imported bananas. Kempthorne sees h^2 as an imaginary number on the
grounds of which no reasonable expectation can be made, for example, about
the effectiveness of compensation programs.

The geneticist, Lewontin[3], states approximately the same. Genetically
seen the question is, according to him, almost impossible to answer because
we do not know anything about the genotype of intelligence, and more or less
direct observations of mechanisms, cross-breeding experiments, and such are
impossible in practice. If Jensen says that dumb children can scarcely be
trained because of the genetic basis of their IQ, this is in conflict with
the rapid increase of height and average life duration which should have
just as much to do with heredity. Lewontin adds that at congresses
geneticists never speak about this topic because they feel that the question
is meaningless, and therefore he terminates with the pronouncement: "The
problem of assaying the genetic component of IQ test differences seems

utterly trivial and hardly worth the immense effort that would need to be
expended to carry out decent studies."

Angrier still are the biologists Medawar and Medawar[4] who say:
"Geneticism is a word that has been coined to describe the enthusiastic
misapplication of not fully understood genetic principles in situations to
which they do not apply. IQ psychologists are among its most advanced
practitioners."

The astronomer, Layzer[5], who has been quoted earlier, contends that
psychology does itself no good by giving circular or operational definitions
of intelligence, and that we must commence with theory and not with
measuring.

A Soup Theory

During the last few years work has been put into the development of a
theory about intelligence based on the interaction of parents and children
and children mutually within families. In the past it was repeatedly
observed that first-born children are over-represented in higher occupational groups. Whether that has something to do with intelligence as such is
not known; a simple explanation can be that with only and oldest children
a relatively large percentage of the family income is spent on education.
Children who are born later consequently climb less and are therefore also
somewhat less intelligent. Van Heek et al.[6] object that parents in choosing
schools will not completely disregard the possibilities of their other
children. It would apply, however, that successful labourers children
(indeed) stem mainly from small families. However, it can be defended that
precisely those parents who value education keep their family small. In
particular, in families of white-collar workers there is little difference
in streaming of the children to higher education as a function of the number
of children. Although the streaming between children of blue and white-
collar workers differs strongly, the influence of the average family size is
relatively small, much too small in any case to be able to reasonably
explain the discrepancy. Irrespective of family size the streaming
opportunity of the oldest child is relatively high, according to Van Heek,
which applies to a much lesser degree with families of more than 4 children.
These connections are therefore not entirely clear.

The Raven Progressive Matrices Test, among others, is used from the
end of the second World War by the Dutch military to estimate the intel-

ligence of the recruits. Their condition is expressed in the so-called
ABOHZIS which is a Dutch abbreviation for general condition, upper body,
lower body, hearing, sight, intelligence and (emotional) stability. Per
category, a five-point scale with unequal percentages is commonly employed
whereby it applies that 1 related to the highest 10% of the concerned
distribution and 5 to the lowest 10%. Therefore, the ideal military man
has an ABOHZIS of 1111111. It has slowly become a folkloristic custom to
burst out in tears or something similar during the examination which leads
to an S5, as a result of which one is no longer eligible.

Regarding intelligence scores, an old study of Idenburg and Zeegers[7]
looked at all kinds of things using, amongst others, 65,363 boys who passed
the draft examination of 1952. They found that the IQ of a recruit is
inclined to come out lower in proportion to the number of children in the
family from which he originates. This would therefore mean that intelligence and family size are negatively correlated, whereby it must be noted
that data about the scores of girls are missing. Further, different
regions in the country appeared to show highly divergent average IQ's a
phenomenon that can perhaps be partly traced back to the family size. An
example: of recruits originating from parts in the south of Holland only
2.26% attained the highest IQ class, while 26.67% of those who originated
from the area around large cities belonged to this group. The average
family size in the south was considerably greater than in the neighbourhood
of cities like The Hague[8].

A few American researchers[9] who apparently were not familiar with the
work of Idenburg et al. studied this themselves. They collected the Raven
scores of 386,114 boys who were tested between 1963 and 1966 in the Dutch
Navy Recruit Center where the Raven was also used, among other tests. At
first glance this procedure and such a large sample has many advantages. It
is now possible to compare social classes, occupational and educational
levels without being restricted to a few observations. Moreover, everyone
is given the same test of which some feel that this, at least in proportion
to other IQ tests, is reasonably free of schooling influences. Finally,
all specimens of the sample are studied at the same age (18 years).
Especially the latter is an important point because age differences is a
weak point of various, much smaller, foreign studies.

The authors have divided the data in two ways. Three occupational
groups are distinguished: white-collar workers, blue-collar workers, and
those active in the agricultural sector. The tendency is that the average

intelligence decreases in this order which in first instance does not have
to cause little amazement, in view of the schooling. The second division
regards IQ as a function of the birth order and the family size (from 1 to
9 children). The average intelligence demonstrates the inclination to
decrease with family size. This effect is rather pronounced with the blue-
collar workers and somewhat less pronounced with the white-collar workers.
With the agrarian occupations family size scarcely plays a role. All groups
show that intelligence decreases with the birth order, that is, the second
child is dumber than the first, the third scores somewhat lower than the
second, etc. Further, it applies that the decline is quite high with the
last child of most family sizes. Figure 10 illustrates the results of the
complete sample[10].

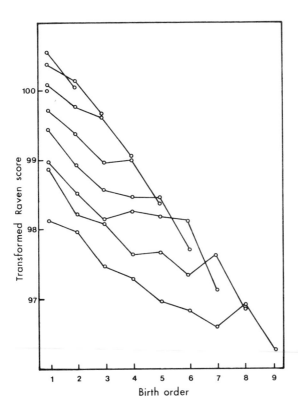

Figure 10 Intelligence scores as a function of family size and birth order.

Five phenomena appear observable:
1. The average intelligence decreases with family size.
2. Intelligence decreases with birth order.
3. Especially in larger families the decline of the last child is relatively large.
4. The speed of the decline as a function of the birth order decreases
   somewhat as the family size increases.
5. The only child is an exception insofar that he does not score the
   highest.

Neither the genetic nor environmental theories can easily describe these
phenomena. Zajonc and Markus have conceived a "confluence model" based on
social psychology that could perhaps be best described as a "soup theory".
They assume that intelligence is determined by the interaction of all
family members mutually, therefore including the parents. The environment
is not a factor which is passively imprinted on the child, but the child is
a part of his own environment, contributes to it, and is influenced in turn.
The authors suppose that in a family there is something like an "intellectual
climate". Unfortunately we are left in uncertainty about the question asking
what precisely must be understood here. Perhaps conversation level, language
usage, or something similar can be thought of. Maybe one family settles
themselves around the tube every evening after glancing reticently at
magazine pictures, while the neighbours play "Das Wohltempierte Klavier"
six-handedly, and correct with pencil the strange modulations made by the
composer, after which a discussion is held about the possible terrible
implications of the DNA recombinant studies using the latest edition of the
Encyclopedia Brittanica.

Zajonc and Markus in any case express the intellectual climate in
numbers. Assume that the contribution of the father is called 100 and that
of the mother is 100 as well, then the intellectual soup of the pair is
averaged at 100. If a child is born, this has consequences for the intellectual soup. The child does not play piano immediately and also does not
pose difficult questions, but does require much time and attention for
elementary care. Initially the contribution is defined as nil so that the
climate is equal to $100 + 100 + 0 : 3 = 67$. However, the child grows up and
brings in his own contribution. Assume that the level of 20 is reached and
that the following child is born. In that case the situation becomes $100 +
+ 100 + 20 + 0 : 4 = 55$. This means that the second child lives in thinner
intellectual soup and (consequently?) develops himself less quickly and

highly. With the following child the situation can be 100 + 100 + 30 + 20 + + 0 : 5 = 50 which means a further deterioration for the family as a whole and especially for the newly born child. It is clear in this line of thought that the intellectual level of a family must be higher as the number of children is smaller. An example follows to indicate that the time between successive births is of importance. With a family of two children and a pause of, for example, 15 years the situation could be 100 + 100 + 100 + 0 : 4 = 75. The "afterthought" is therefore better off than the first child who initially had to be satisfied with 100 + 100 + 0 : 3 = 67. With the aid of (hypothetical) growth curves Zajonc and Markus attempt to say something about optimal time distances between (a number of) children.

The vicissitudes of multiple births are interesting in this context. It has been observed that the average IQ of twins is 95, that of triplets 90, etc. From both the nature as well as the environmental theory there is little to be said about this but the soup theory can provide a solution. The environment of triplets is 100 + 100 + 0 + 0 + 0 : 5 = 40, that of twins is 50, therefore worse for the intellectual development. If one of a pair of twins is still-born it must allow a "better" milieu for the living child in this train of thought (67 if the twins were from a first pregnancy), and the IQ of those children would indeed be normal on the average.

However, two factors cannot be easily explained. The only child is associated with an optimal environment but nevertheless does not score the highest, and the last child often demonstrates a relatively considerable decline. Zajonc and Markus presume that this is because children become more intelligent if they have the opportunity to explain things to their brothers and sisters. This possibility is lacking for an only child and is also scarcely present with the last child.

Problems

It is clear that there are rather some problems with both the data as well as with this theory. To begin with, the dispersion in figure 10 does look impressive, but it only concerns approximately 1.4% of the population variance, or rather 3 IQ points, while the measurement error of tests is larger as a rule. Therefore, we can ask ourselves what it is that we are actually talking about. Further, it is not unthinkable that younger children (boys) in a family are less motivated to do well on the test. A number of them hope for exemption owing to their brother's service and others perhaps

have heard few enthusiastic stories from brothers who have served. It is
also possible that birth complications increase with the number of children
and that the physiological state of the mother during pregnancy as a result
of both her increasing age as well as the fact that she can have little
rest because of the growing family, becomes steadily worse in the course of
the time. Perhaps the dip of the last child could have something to do with
the end of a series of complications with the birth of the children.
Moreover, it is not clear why it is that only children appear to go far in
the world, but this remark is actually superfluous because we are almost
talking about a fraction of an IQ point. A phenomenon which does not seem
to fit at all in the theory is that the youngest children from larger
families receive a higher education on the average than the oldest children
from the same family[11].

About Negroes, Birth Rates, and Broken Families

Zajonc[12] also looked at other material that could have something to do
with his theory. In America approximately the same phenomena occur as with
us. Also in France and Scotland the average intelligence decreases with
family size, but IQ becomes *higher* there as a function of birth order.
Zajonc presumes that this is related to the average time between successive
births. The birth rates in these countries are considerably lower and the
pause between the successive children is longer on the average. However,
this explains at the most that the decline within the family would elapse
less quickly but not that IQ increases. The theory further predicts that
children in families with one parent (widow, widower, divorced, etc.) will
have a lower IQ, which would indeed be the case. Regarding the race
differences and the relatively low-scoring negro, Zajonc remarks that the
birth rate is higher with negroes than with whites and that the intervals
between the children are smaller. Moreover, it would occur relatively more
in a negro family that the father does not reside at home so that his
contribution is lacking. That boys score higher on some tests than girls is,
explains Zajonc, because the average time that elapses between the birth of
boys is longer than that between girls, which can be partly traced back to
the fact that relatively more boys are stillborn. Also, school performance
differs considerably in various countries, which he ascribes as well to the
birth rate. Zajonc discovered that children in Iran are relatively dumb and
that the country has a much higher birth rate than Western Europe. Here the

writer goes rather far: in similar (underdeveloped) countries more important causes can be pointed out for insufficient schooling. Finally, a few remarks about adoption are interesting. The adoption of a child brings along with it that the foster family *changes*. It must be said that so far this possibility has not been thought of. The theory also predicts that the IQ of MZ and DZ twins must be equal and about that are in any case some doubts.

Conclusion

The opinions about interaction between nature and environment consist, on the one side, of strong objections against such a simple division and, on the other side - for the time being - of a weak impulse for a theory which must serve to explain intelligence differences from micro-social variables. Although it can perhaps be said that a movement has been started in this direction, the results so far have not been very spectacular and convincing. Moreover, as good as nothing is known about the nature of the interactions within the family that would lead to the differences and everything rotates around this in the end.

Footnotes, Chapter 7

1. Anastasi (1976)
2. Kempthorne (1978); his calculation examples are technically incorrect.
3. Lewontin (1975)
4. Medawar and Medawar (1977)
5. Layzer (1972), see also Cleary et al. (1975)
6. Van Heek et al. (1972)
7. Idenburg and Zeegers (1951, 1957)
8. We will consider this further in chapter 9.
9. Belmont and Marolla (1973)
10. Zajonc and Markus (1975)
11. Nienhuys (1979) has serious statistical objections against the theory
    of Zajonc and Markus. See also Van Heek (1972)
12. Zajonc (1976)

8 MILIEU AND COMPENSATION PROGRAMS

The moment has arrived for us to ask ourselves what the terms "milieu" and "environment" mean. Also here it applies that words are sometimes swifter than thoughts, because many appear to say, when asked, that milieu is the whole of influencing factors. Therefore, a tautology. Subsequently, the question will be asked how something like milieu can be studied and what this has resulted in. Finally, the question arises whether behaviour, in this case intelligence, can be influenced from the environment.

A Bag Full of Atoms and a Skewed Distribution

Man can be described and studied on a number of organizational levels. As extremes, a bag full of atoms of raw elements can be conceived of on the one hand, which seem to be worth approximately one dollar and, on the other hand, the spiritual self-actualizer who is partly supernatural, because Binswanger already said: "Die Liebe geht über die Welt hinaus". Usually the physiological or psychological organizational level is chosen. The determining factors lie, as is said, more with internal and genetic processes than environmental variables. Intelligence and intelligence differences can also be seen and perhaps influenced from these angles. Striving for more equality of possibilities and (educational) opportunities is central here.

If the distribution of IQ is taken as the point of departure, three possibilities can be conceived of. The first is that attempts are made to shift the whole distribution in terms of raw scores, and in such a way that the population becomes more intelligent on the whole. That has occurred (unwittingly) in the last century in the framework of the introduction of compulsory education and the founding of countless schools and courses. However, the differences between people have remained about the same, which is a thorn in the flesh of the egalitarianists who aim mainly for more equality of incomes and who see intelligence and schooling, among other

137

things, as a road to this. According to them, differences can be diminished
by providing extra schooling to those with a low IQ, or to improve the
upbringing, The distribution of the IQ would become skewed because of this,
although the test constructer can solve that. Strictly taken, a third
variant implies that the distribution loses both tails. This means that
compensation programs are conceived of and executed, and very improper
schools are founded which are compulsory for those who threaten to become
talented.

The second possibility is central in the so-called environmental
theory; the last has not been executed yet. The left tail of the IQ
distribution is eligible for "catching up" programs, that is, less talented
children, and eventually demented senior citizens.

Learning Pills

If the word "environment" is interpreted broadly enough (everything
that influences an organism), physiological variables also belong to the
milieu. Effects of undernourishment were discussed previously. Another
possibility consists of medicinal interventions. In this case, biologists
and pharmacists have lately worked, sometimes in teamwork with industry, on
compounds which would work as an intelligence increaser and which are sometimes called learning pills.

The nervous system is closely connected with the endocrine system (the
hormones) both anatomically as well as functionally. There are disputes
about the question as to which gland can be called the "master gland".
Until recently this role was ascribed to the hypophysis or pituitary gland;
some conjecture that the epiphysis (pineal gland) is even more important.
In any case, the pituitary gland produces a large number of hormones that
directly affect the organs, or that regulates the activity of other
endocrine glands[1]. One of the compounds is abbreviated as ACTH and
influences the activity of the adrenal gland which in turn produces so-
called stress hormones (corticosteriodes) which are needed to raise alert-
ness, combat infection reactions, and so on. It is also presumed that these
compounds stimulate centers in the brain, directly or indirectly, which
have to do with emotions. A second hormone of the pituitary gland is
vasopressin which has, among other things, a vascularstricture influence.
A third substance that plays a role in certain metabolic processes in the
brain (not a hormone) is piracetam.

It was discovered that rats whose pituitary gland had been removed were no longer capable of learning, which did not apply to people after an operation on account of a pituitary gland tumour. Attention was drawn to ACTH consisting of a chain of 39 amino acids. Chemically, four up to and including nine or ten amino acids (ACTH 4-9 or 4-10) were cut out of the molecule. Studies of rats suggested that these fragments directly effectuated something in the brain, therefore without intervention from the adrenal gland. If a rat is administered an electric shock shortly after a light flash or a sound, the animal will jump away from the dangerous spot (avoidance conditioning). If the shock is omitted the rat unlearns that behaviour (extinction). However, if the animals are given parts of ACTH they demonstrate the avoidance behaviour longer. Therefore, their memory appears to have improved.

In another experiment rats run through a maze in search of food. Also here it applies that behaviour shows extinction if no (more) food appears to be available. Administering ACTH demonstrates, however, that the animal will keep trying.

If a rat has learned something and receives an electric shock the result is memory loss, just as with man in a psychiatric institution. The amnesia appeared to be cured more rapidly if the rats were provided with ACTH fragments or a part of the vasopressin molecule. On the grounds of these and similar tests the conjecture arose that some drugs cause motivation or directly improve memory.

It is clear that such animal studies, resting on very simple learning processes, provide no explanation about human behaviour. In the first place, it can be noted that the adherence to avoidance behaviour (perseverance) actually means that useless actions are being remembered. On the grounds of that it can be defended that the learning pill makes the animal *dumber* unless it is decided that useless behaviour is intelligent. A more important point is that human learning presumably rests on a hierarchy of processes, from being conditioned up to and including the deciphering of modern poetry, a hierarchy holding that not all forms of learning can be described or explained from one set of laws (compare chapter 2). From this point of view experiments with humans are therefore worth considering and this has also amply occurred, whether or not at the request of the pharmaceutical industry[2]. To assure that the results are not influenced by expectations which subjects and experimenters eventually have, such a study must occur "double blind". This means that nobody knows who received the actual

substance and who received the placebo. The results with a number of
students as volunteers can be summarized as follows:

ACTH has no influence on the ability to memorize word pairs. It also
appears that no better performance was produced in the area of so-called
functional learning, whereby attempts must be made to discover a mathematical function when a series of numbers is presented. Also, a part of an
intelligence test in the area of abstract thinking demonstrated no progress.
The only exception was a test where reaction times were registered over a
long time period. Under the influence of ACTH a smaller number of errors
were gradually made than the control group, and extremes in the form of
long reaction times occurred less frequently. The conclusion of the
researchers is that the expression "learning pill" is improperly chosen.
The only thing that can be said about ACTH is that the substance presumably
works as a stimulant and a motivation-increaser, just as a reprimanding
address or a strong cup of coffee.

Studies of senior citizens were done with piracetam. The substance was
discovered by accident in 1963 as a remedy against motion sickness, and
appeared (besides this) to somewhat improve the oxygen supply of the brain
(for animals). Experiments with rats demonstrated approximately the same as
ACTH and vasopressin fragments.

Diesfeldt et al.[3] report that various researchers would have encountered positive effects with people. The authors, however, have much criticism
against these studies. Sometimes a control group was lacking, the subject
populations were no properly comparable, etc. During their own research
that took ten months, they scaled 35 behavioural dimensions with an
experimental and a control group. This experiment appears to be set-up well:
a double blind procedure was used, subjects were chosen with an equal starting level regarding a number of aspects of their functioning, and standard-
ized, reliable, behaviour tests were used instead of the "clinical
impressions" so often praised in medical circles. Piracetam had no positive
effects but in a few cases unpleasant side-effects appeared such as unrest
and agitation.

A large study with piracetam was further performed by Meertens[4]. In a
few nursing homes senior citizens were selected who suffered from minor
dementia. This manifested itself in a defective imprinting ability of
recent occurrences, poor concentration, disorientation in place and time,
changing moods, and capricious behaviour. The population was split into two
groups. All performed a large number of tests in the area of short-term

memory for pictures and numbers, recognition of words and pictures,
concentration ability, calculating, reaction time, cooperation between eye
and hand in the execution of movements. the perception of figure and background, seeing spatial relations, orientation in place and time, and spatial
imaginative faculty. Finally, a list was used upon which many behaviours of
everyday life were scaled. When it appeared that the groups had an almost
equal starting level, and were therefore comparable, the one half was
administered piracetam daily for three months and the other a placebo
(double blind).

After three months nothing appeared to have changed, at least not for
the good. Meertens' conclusions does not lie about this: "When the
pharmaceutical industry presumes that these functions improve it takes a
step which, as appears from the performed studies, is not supported by
scientific research." It may cause amazement that the Dutch Index of
Packaged Medicines nevertheless mentions piracetam the last few years under
the trade name Nootropil (presumably Greek for "aiming at the mind"). In
various editions it is said (in different ways) that Nootropil has no
stimulating effect on motor ability, and that presumably the processes which
have to do with learning and memorizing, or with the integration of higher
psychic functions (whatever that might mean) are improved. This is rather
strange because the study has showed the *opposite* here and there (agitation)
and, moreover, improved learning and memorizing is not apparent. It is to
be hoped that other medicines which are brought on the market are based on
research that can withstand the test of criticism[5].

What is Environment?

We will now look at interventions of a psychological nature. If intelligence is to be influenced via manipulation of the environment, the first
and most important question is which environmental factors are essential
for the cognitive development. Literature is available in this area. A
horrible example is a large scale study of Broman et al.[6]

The authors gathered 65 so-called predictor variables. These considered prenatal influences, neonatal vicissitudes, and the psychic development
in an early phase. Since the authors possessed no unnecessarily complicated
theory, a broad range of possibilities was chosen. Some are the number of
X-rays that were ever made of the mother, her smoking habits, eventual
anaemia during the pregnancy, the audibility of heart tones immediately
prior to the delivery, the number of visits to the doctor, the weight of

the placenta, the height and the head circumference of the child, the weight
after 4 months, eventual congenital heart disease and brain damage, the
quality of eye movements after 1 year, and the Apgar score[7]. These are
correlated with the IQ of 26,751 children, neatly divided into black and
white, boys and girls. The combined 65 variables appear to be responsible
for 20% of the IQ variance, whereby the authors apprehensively conclude that
brain damage and intelligence have something to do with each other, but that
this does not apply to negro girls.

    Dissatisfaction with the results led to the study being repeated with
169 variables and 26,760 children. Fearing that they might forget something
they added the length of the menstrual cycle, the blood group, the number
of attempts required to get pregnant (?), fever during pregnancy, the
composition of the urine of the mother, use of the forceps, yellow
complexion of the child, temperature in the first year of life, and not
lastly the colour of the meconium, or rather the first stool of the baby.
The result hardly brought anything more to light. Still, this approach does
offer perspectives. What is stopping us from creating a "think tank", with
the aid of unemployed psychologists, who think up a thousand of such
variables to test a million children? Computers are large and fast enough.
If the air pressure seems to be of importance, then the mother can always
be told to change this on time.

    This study, however, exposes a serious problem, namely that we do not
know what environment is. Even if h^2 would not be a meaningless figure and
its value is .80, then people with a genotypic IQ of 100 can still always
change 40 points[8]. The question is therefore what factors effectuate that.
Jensen[9] mentions an old study of Burks from which it would appear that a
maximally favourable or unfavourable environment (within reasonable
boundaries) could make a difference of 26 IQ points. According to him, the
intelligence of the parents is essential (especially the mother) which co-
varies with the amount of time devoted to reading aloud, helping with homework, and such. Jensen says further that extreme changes of the environment
can cause as much as 70 points difference. As an example he mentions a child
of a deaf and dumb mother who had an IQ of 30 at the age of 6 years, and 100
at the age of 8 (also compare figure 4). Bereiter[10] claims that the relation
between cognitive development and milieu is not linear, but has threshold
effects. Income, housing, and reading books would be variables that do not
matter much above a certain level, but which are responsible for considerable differences under that.

    Scarr and Weinberg[11] concentrated on negro children who were adopted

by whites which would change many (social) circumstances. The foster parents
had an IQ of one standard deviation above the average of the biological
parents, and they belonged to a higher social class. The adopted children
received a higher IQ after some time and the authors state that all negroes
would score 10 to 20 points extra if they were treated in a comparable
manner. Stein and Susser[12] conclude in a review article that systematically
a not inconsiderable change in IQ is certainly possible, and can be reached
by placing children in a better social milieu and creating better circumstances. The effect of stimulation would be the most spectacular for severe-
ly disadvantaged groups. An increase of 30 points would also have been
observed in kibbutzes[13].

Husén[14] says that we are still far removed from tracking down the
relevant family and upbringing factors, at least aside from clichés such as
social class, income, occupation, and status where correlations do exist
but which do not further provide any insight. He feels that IQ and schooling have less to do with financial than with motivational thresholds. The
strongest influence would not be intellectual but motivational. It mainly
concerns interested parents who encourage their children. The multiple
correlation between things such as the degree of stimulation, allowing the
children to read books, the availability of their own room, and the IQ,
would be approximately .70 and the correlation with report card marks higher still. Also, longitudinal studies about the vicissitudes of children
would have proved this. The care and the devotion of the parents are,
according to Husén, of great importance, such as for example their inclination to attend school meetings, which would occur less with the lower
classes. Others[15] claim approximately the same. From a Swedish longitudinal
study it comes to the foreground that occupational success has much more to
do with the sphere at home, health, and ambition than with the (original)
IQ. The correlation between the IQ of the child and the occupational level
of the parents climbs with the years, which is ascribed to the treatment
at home, available reading material, expectations regarding schooling, and
so on. Tyler feels further that IQ is not so much a cause of learning but
is more a result of cumulative learning processes. This leads us to the
question what various educational interventions have shown so far.

Problems

There are a few statistical and methodological tricks that could play

a role in compensation programs. The first is regression toward the mean
(see chapter 4) that arises when subjects are chosen who score extremely
low, in relation to the average of their population, and insufficient
measures are taken to compile a good control group. In the second place, a
strange phenomenon can occur if groups are split. A made up example:

	higher IQ	equal IQ	amount	percent improved
Boys				
intervention	18	12	30	60
no intervention	7	3	10	70
Girls				
intervention	2	8	10	20
no intervention	9	21	30	30
Total				
intervention	20	20	40	50
no intervention	16	24	40	40

In this case the experimental and control group consist of 40 children, but
the amounts regarding the gender is unequally distributed over the conditions. Inspection of the results of both sub-groups creates the impression
that the educational intervention makes the children dumber; the table
demonstrating the total shows the opposite.

Jensen[16] remarks that the profit of compensation programs is greater as
the age of commencement is lower. He ascribes that to, this time statistically interpreted, regression toward the mean, and rightfully so because the
test-retest correlation is very low with young children, so that we expect
a large "profit" only on the grounds of this unreliability with extreme
scorers.

Further, care must be taken that the test does not measure the skills
that are already learned. With intelligence a score should be concerned
that also ought to be transferrable to *other* skills and situations.

Discomfort regarding the test situation can also play a role. Jensen
mentions as an example a child who attained a profit of 10 IQ points after
being put at ease for awhile by playing with finger paint. Then there is
the (theoretical) problem that parents who voluntarily expose their child to
compensation programs would be somewhat more motivated than the control
group. It is conceivable that they change their behaviour at home in relation
to the child and in such a way that effects emerge from this which the
researcher in question ascribes to his interventions at school. This could

perhaps be avoided by compiling a control group from children who apply but
are not admitted. Also, diffusion of the experimental to the control group
is conceivable. This holds that the control children adapt all sorts of
games and such from the experimental group without the experimenter's
knowledge, with the possible result that the intervention demonstrates
little difference.

Compensation Programs

The idea behind the compensation programs is contrary to the philosophy
of predetermined development (see chapter 1). Before the second World War
there was no thought given to expanding developmental psychology to a large
extent by attempting to change the encountered phenomena[17]. The great
amounts of refugees who appeared to develop very slowly were, however, a
reason to start thinking differently. An inducement in America caused the
Civil Rights Movement, and the so-called Sputnik shock in 1957 when it
appeared that the Russians were a few steps ahead in space travel, after
which a need arose for the fostering of more talent. Only concerning the
United States this already consisted of billion dollar programs such as
Head Start, the Banneker Project, Higher Horizons, etc.[18]

In 1967 a report was published by the U.S. Commission on Civil Rights.
The drift[19] was that hardly any effects were encountered. In many cases a
profit was reported from 5 to 10 IQ points but these disappeared in the
course of time. As positive points it was mentioned that various medical
defects were discovered on time and that the motivation of the children and
their attitude towards the school and schooling in general were positively
influenced. This brought Jensen to the well-known passage: "Compensatory
education has been tried and it apparently has failed". Jensen asks himself
whether the compensation programs work as a hot-house or as fertilizer. The
first means that a flower blossoms sooner, but not prettier or better. He
feels that this can be attained with children insofar that simple associative
relations such as 1 + 1 = 2 can be learned at an earlier age, but according
to him there is no transference to higher cognitive abilities. Only extremely well-defined partial achievements would be improved. The comparison with
fertilizer means that a larger crop results, or rather that the IQ of the
population is permanently increased. According to Jensen, this will not
succeed and that is caused by the genetic determination of intelligence
differences[20].

It is clear that this study has some rather (politically tinted) implications and is of interest to various scientific researchers. Many groups seem to have objections against compensation programs (afterwards?) that are sustained by the (apparently) negative results[21]. According to some of its practitioners[22], sociology is characterized by lack of a theory and the posing of interesting questions, so that one is restricted to criticizing others. Anyway, sociologists remark that compensation programs discriminate between population groups. Psycholinguists note that the influencing of vocabulary and language usage does not yet imply a change in thinking. Some pedagogues still maintain that the child mainly receives and ought to receive his developmental impulses from within, so that interventions are harmful. Educationalists often find the programs too detailed. The critical psychologists feel that it is wrong to force something onto the working class, and the nature theory curtly explains that it is only a waste of money.

In any case, five questions can be posed about compensation-intended education:

1. Can IQ indeed be increased?
2. What happens to the level after the intervention?
3. When is intervention the most effective?
4. What type of program is the best?
5. Which children profit the most?

An actual question at issue, which still has to do with the idea of predetermined development, holds that there is a dispute about the time of commencement, and whether the effects of early "deprivation" can be caught up with later. Animal experiments with cats, dogs, and rats created the suggestion that detriments sustained early can hardly be made up for, which is expressed in the anecdotes about the wolf children. Clarke and Clarke[23] express many doubts concerning this. They do not strongly believe in the importance of critical periods for cognitive development, and note that early intervention is a precarious undertaking insofar that the predictive value of IQ tests with young children is extremely slight anyway. Therefore, profit or loss says little in the long run, where it can be added that the evaluation of compensation programs, strangely enough, as a rule has taken place over only a few years. If one commences with children aged two or three years and their IQ is studied before school age, no justifiable conclusion can be drawn, per definition (compare the Berkeley Growth Study, chapter 3).

The idea of an early start is especially defended by Bloom[24] who says that, preeminently, interventions must be made in the phase where many developments occur most rapidly. However, he does not make the rationale of this clear and, moreover, Bloom's reasoning is unsound. He concludes from the low correlations of growth studies, among others, that early age goes together with the most "plastic" nervous system. Low correlations and a susceptible nervous system, hoewever, do not need to have anything to do with each other; it is very well possible that the low figures originate from the comparison of incomparable tests, which is caused in turn by the fact that we do not know what intelligence (with children) is.

In any case, this reasoning was the inducement to begin with younger children after the limited success of the program Head Start, that was especially aimed at lower school age. Bronfenbrenner[25] says that the largest profit is to be expected from properly constructed cognitive programs (whatever they may be) whereby, however, the socially and economically weakest profit the least. This would mean therefore that the interventions work preeminently with children for whom they were not meant in the first place. Further, the interaction between parents and children throughout the whole day would be of the greatest importance, meaning that a few hours of education outside the home has little effect. Programs that mainly take place in the home and where the teacher, moreover, regularly visits the family, would be the most fruitful and the profit is then also maintained the longest. In this way one standard deviation of the IQ (15 points) would be attainable. Also, Bronfenbrenner feels that one can almost not start early enough.

Riksen-Walraven[26] says that an intensive program from the age of three months to six years can produce some 30 IQ points. Others[27] performed a study with 40 newly-born children whose mothers had an IQ of less than 70. The population was randomly divided into an experimental and a control group. The first was exposed to intervention from the age of two weeks, whereby both the children as well as the mothers were virtually trained the whole day long in many areas. At the age of 5.5 years the children had an average IQ of more than 120, that of the controls was 94, which must have had something to do with the regression toward the mean.

Kohnstamm et al.[28] have quite some criticism about many studies that have produced positive results. Between 1970 and 1975 they worked in Amsterdam with an experimental day nursery where the children could come for whole or half days. The program consisted of countless games and language and social development training; also motor ability, creativity, and musical

ability were not omitted. The parents were involved with the program via
regular discussions and the lending of toys. The experimental group consisted of children between 1 and 3 years of age, originating from families with
short (SS) and long schooling (LS). Enrolling LS children did not appear to
be a problem, but it was difficult to find SS parents who were interested.
The background of forming an LS group was that milieu-blending could perhaps
be possible and helpful and, moreover, there was a curiosity about eventual
differences between SS and LS after the end of the experimental period. The
children could remain at the day nursery until their fourth birthday; the
different ages and the fact that some children visited the nursery half a
day and the others whole days made it possible to bring the degree of
eventual changes into context with the duration of their visit.

There were no clear hypotheses. On the one side, it was presumed that
children who were behind would learn much in the nursery, because where
there is little there is room for much more. On the other side, it was
supposed that advanced children would learn the most. The children (and
naturally the control group) were first studied with tests such as the
Bayley. Suspicion against the test and a fear of statistical regression
later led to the choice of simply LS and SS as a criterion. In the course
of time, tests were taken such as again the Bayley, the Stanford-Binet,
language level tests, vocabulary tests, etc. The LS group had a higher IQ at
the outset. On leaving the nursery the IQ of the LS was 18 points higher on
the average, with the SS children it was only 4 points. The number of years
spent at the nursery did not make much difference, no more than the question
whether the children had been present for whole or half days. After
attending kindergarten for a year both groups had basically lost their lead.
They did, however, show more independent behaviour, more assertiveness and,
in general, a change in attitude towards others and elders. The project was
(consequently) viewed as a failure for an important part. About the reasons
for this little is known, and also because the researchers themselves were
groping in the dark about the measures they had to invent to increase IQ.
Further, there are naturally problems with the tests and their reliability.
On page 185 the authors write something strange in this respect: "Although
little is known about the validity of these tests, we have no reason to
doubt the validity of these instruments of measure." How can one in ignorance
not have doubts?

Habituation

A theoretically well-thought out attempt is made by Riksen-Walraven[29].
Also she points out that numerous "massive enrichment" programs only have a
temporary effect, and links to this that lacking a theory you actually do
not know what you are doing in such a case. She reports further that tests in
the preverbal period have no predictive value and are, moreover, unreliable.

Her approach is based on experimental psychology and psychophysiology.
One of the basic cognitive faculties is the recognition of people, objects,
and situations. The problem with young children is that they can express
little in words. There are, however, other means to come to know something
about cognitive processes.

If a stimulus is new and/or unexpected a so-called orientation reaction
(OR) occurs in man and animal. This holds that the pupils dilate, the
auditory thresholds drop, the head is turned in the direction of the
stimulus source, various motor activity stops, vascular dilation occurs in
the head (and the brain), respiration becomes slower and deeper, heart rate
becomes less frequent and/or irregular, and the electrical resistance of the
skin (GSR) temporarily decreases. Such phenomena are interpreted as an
attempt of the organism to maximally admit information. If the same stimulus
is presented repeatedly habituation occurs, which contains that the strength
of the mentioned reactions decreases. An example is the ticking of a clock
that, after a time, is not heard anymore. Some suppose that habituation has
to do with the forming of a so-called "neural model" of the stimulus
(Solokov), therefore a piece of brain mythology. Habituation means that not
much attention is paid to the stimuli, as a result of which, among other
things, small changes are perceived less well. Sight becomes, so to speak,
filtered by knowledge.

With small children the OR as well as heart rate deceleration with new
stimuli also occurs, just as habituation. The OR is viewed as accompanying
phenomena of processes which are on a low cognitive level. It is rather
difficult to study this with new-born children because they must then be
pasted full of electrodes. A simpler measure is the time that a child looks
at a picture, for instance. The fixation duration would have something to
do with the information processing and with the quality of the built-up
model. With older children there is a correlation between heart rate
deceleration and fixation duration, which should therefore point out that
the viewing time may indeed be seen as a measure for habituation and

information processing. With simple pictures the habituation rate increases with age, through which the processing of increasingly complicated stimulus patterns becomes possible. There are differences in habituation rate between children which may perhaps be seen as measures for the ability to execute elementary cognitive operations. At a later age the correlation between habituation rate and concept formation is .37. The speed at the age of 4 months further correlates positively with IQ tests which are taken at 14 months, and the correlation between habituation rate at the age of 1 year and the Binet IQ at 44 months would be .48. As a further indication in this direction it is mentioned that there is also a positive relation with the Apgar score.

The hypotheses of the study contained the following. More stimulation of younger children means more opportunity to habituate, with all the gratifying results for later IQ. There would be a correlation of .55 between the habituation rate and the degree to which the mother laughs at, touches, talks to the child, etc. From the age of approximately 1 year an average difference in habituation rate is revealed by children from different milieus. The tempo is the highest with the higher social classes. This could, therefore, be related to the upbringing. According to Riksen-Walraven it applies that parents from lower milieus do stimulate the child satis-factorily and provide toys, but that the stimulation, especially regarding toys and looking at pictures, is rather uniform (a hundred cars in the box). Higher classes would put a more varied repertoire into behaviour. Stimulation of the child is, therefore, obvious. A second facet is that the children tend to be active themselves; they cannot only *be* stimulated but also *search* for stimulation. Also in this respect, individual differences exist. Especially in the lower milieus the exploration urge would be scarce-ly encouraged, with the possible result that one later hardly realizes that it is possible to influence the environment, which again has negative consequences for the aspiration level, among other things. This can be seen with apathetic institutionalized children. Similar adaptation to the child's own activity is referred to as the degree of responsiveness of the mother. This would also be stronger in the higher classes. Parents who belonged to the lower strata believe, as a manner of speaking, in the theory of pre-destined development; they therefore have a nothing-can-be-done-about-it mentality resulting in a rather resigned upbringing. In turn, this has consequences for the idea that the child himself later develops about the possibilities of taking the initiative. Further, the mother often finds it awkward to communicate with the child and therefore refrains from that to a certain extent, through which the child scarcely communicates with her and with the environment, and by which the circle is closed.

The study was aimed at 4 times 25 parent-child pairs originating from the lower social milieus. At the pretest the children were 9 months old and the program lasted 3 months. Schematically, the four conditions were as follows: Responsiveness (R)

		no	yes
Stimulation (S)	no	C	R
	yes	S	SR

The S program meant that the parent stimulated the child more, the R program that the initiative of the child was central, with SR both the first as well as the second occurred, and C was the control group. The S program demonstrated that the habituation rate increased, but that did not apply to the exploration urge. With SR there was also a higher habituation rate, but the R program did not lead to any change in this respect. Habituation speed and exploration urge would (could) therefore be independent dimensions with young children. The S and SR programs were followed by more exploration so that with the last type of intervention the largest effects were observed. Division of the results showed that certainly not only the "better" children profited from the program, but that also initially very slow habituators and children who showed little initiative improved considerably.

It is clear that, in any case, this concerns an original study that however demonstrates a serious shortage, namely the lack of an aftertest. Consequently, we know nothing about the results in the long run.

Conclusion

If one considers cutting off the left tail of the IQ distribution learning pills do not help so far. Manipulation via the environment assumes a theory about cognitive development to a degree which is still insufficiently available. Compensation programs have often only temporary results of which no one is sure why, and if they have permanent success it is also unknown why that is. In any case, it appears that IQ can be improved which, considering the linkage with school and such, in itself is no perplexing information, but the degree to which that works certainly does not plead for the precision of the antipode of the nature theory, namely the idea that only milieu differences lie at the base of IQ ·

Footnotes, Chapter 8

1. See De Wied (1967) for a general survey.
2. Wagenaar (1977), Wagenaar et al. (1977), Gaillard and Sanders (1975), Gaillard and Varey (1977)
3. Diesfeldt et al. (1978)
4. Meertens (1977)
5. Eysenck (1973) recommends the consumption of glutamic acid, which lies in the same area.
6. Broman et al. (1975)
7. The Apgar score is a number that is given to the newborn child and has to do with the general condition such as skin colour (not bluish), respiration, mobility, crying, and such.
8. McCall et al. (1973)
9. Jensen (1972)
10. Bereiter (1970)
11. Scarr and Weinberg (1976)
12. Stein and Susser (1970)
13. For this see a series of articles which were published in the Harvard Educational Review as a reaction to the sensational piece by Jensen (1969).
14. Husén (1975)
15. Tyler (1972)
16. Jensen (1969)
17. Riksen-Walraven (1977)
18. Andriessen et al. (1973)
19. Jensen (1969)
20. Brody and Brody (1976) claim that Jensen in his book (1972) changed his data in 17 places so that his own theory would come out well.
21. Nelissen (1972)
22. See for example Ultee (1977)
23. Clarke and Clarke (1976)
24. Bloom (1974)
25. Bronfenbrenner, in: Montague (1975)
26. Riksen-Walraven (1977)
27. Heber and Garber, in: Brody and Brody (1976)
28. Kohnstamm et al. (1976), see also Rupp (1969)
29. Riksen-Walraven (1977)

Also because psychology has propagated for a long time the instrument of the intelligence test with all its reputed cohesiveness, numerous connections have been made with IQ in both the psychological literature as well as in many types of publications related to education and social policy as a whole. A number of these are suited for further exploration.

Education

There are indications[1] that as a learning process progresses, the rate of learning correlates continually lower with the level of the basic skills. In the course of education the starting level therefore becomes increasingly less important. If this is true, then IQ has a predictive value for the period shortly after taking a test but not in the long run. This phenomenon could also have to do with the low correlations between IQ and occupational success and it is important because, in making decisions about the future of an individual, one test is not sufficient. The latter may, however, be seen more as the rule rather than the exception[2]. Both parents as well as teachers are strengthened by this in their opinion that intelligence is fixed and determines the personal destiny to an important degree. The decisions will often justify themselves.

In the last few years experiments have been carried out about so-called *mastery learning*. This holds that the subject matter is strictly built-up hierarchically. The pupils may begin on level B only if A has been fully mastered. In the beginning, the time that the pupils require to reach a certain level varies with a factor 5, and the correlation with IQ lies between .50 and .70. Therefore, the lower the test results the slower the pupil is. After some time however the tempo differences decrease considerably which naturally leads to a much lower correlation with IQ which then loses its predictive value[3]. Pursuing education is apparently a dynamic process

that is difficult to estimate and predict from one instance. The fact that
a population of children can be divided into IQ classes was a sufficient
justification for many to scarcely think about the processes lying at the
base of the intelligence score, and to hardly think through ideas about
eventual reforming of the educational system or to shove them to the background.

Apart from that there are better predictors of school success to be
found than the IQ test[4]. From year to year the exam results have a
predictive correlation of as high as .80, while the highest predictive
validity that has been encountered with an intelligence test is approximately .70. Moreover, much is to be said for the school results as a whole on
the grounds of performance in the first year, for example, in the form of
the first year of highschool. Also this correlation is approximately .70.
This brings to mind an experiment which is perhaps interesting. The vicissitudes of the indiviual are reliably registered somewhere. Therefore it
must be possible to collect a group of people who have reached the final
phase of their occupation and social class, and to calculate the transition-
al probabilities and correlations with the school results (starting from
elementary school) and the attended schooling. In that case, probably more
can be known than on the grounds of tests, and these can be abolished after
the study with the enjoyable result that much money and manpower becomes
available to pose interesting questions and perform educational experiments.

Husén[5] says that in the civilized countries, in general, compulsory
education exists to the age of 12 years, after which the children are
divided over numerous types of schooling and (later) social classes. He
feels that decisions about the child are taken too soon, and that both the
individual as well as society benefit from a prolonged general education.
Experiments with a special type of secondary schools would have indicated in
a number of countries that these pupils more easily take part in post-
secondary education, which would especially apply to children of manual
labourers. Especially motivational factors seem to be at work here in both
a positive as well as in a negative sense. When the vicissitudes of the
children are followed who belong to the upper third of those taking the
entrance exam for high school and college, a disproportionately large part
from the lower income brackets drop out in the course of time. Husén says
that this phenomenon (thus) has little to do with low intelligence, but all
the more with affective resistance of the parents and children against high-

er education. School performance correlates approximately .35 with social
class. The latter is a strange scale and not lastly because circular reasoning is involved. The highest class is awarded to those who have attended
school the longest, and it is therefore not amazing that in those milieus an
education is given more value. Further, the farmers form a somewhat awkward
category: if various values are ascribed to them the correlation also
naturally changes (is the farmer uneducated, an entrepreneur, or a skilled
labourer?). Husén has also calculated correlations between school performance and the score on a questionnaire which had to do with the views of the
children about their milieu, the relations in the family, the aspiration
level of the parents, and so on. This correlation came out much higher (.70)
than the .35 mentioned with social class, so that he feels that a much too
crude and partly irrelevant index is concerned here. According to him, if
research about the processes which take place within the child and his
environment where intelligence and education are concerned and keeps on
occurring insufficiently, then the numerous correlations will say nothing.

The IQ test also often plays an important role in job applications. For
many applicants the test is a stumbling block which can be described with
the aid of a schema taken from the signal detection theory (a sub-division
of the psychology of perception).

		signal	
		yes	no
answer	yes	hit	false alarm
	no	miss	correct rejection

A signal can be visible on a radar screen and the subject has two possible
answers which lead to four types of events. Two of these are errors and it
appears to be possible in various ways to diminish one of these. Assume that
someone must inspect needles that are intended for record players. A *false
alarm* means that a good needle is rejected which costs the firm money. On
the contrary, a *miss* is worse because the consumer does not like buying a
new needle only to observe afterwards that it horribly scratches his record.
To heavily punish such errors leads to the fact that the needle inspector
applies strict criteria, with the result that also many good needles are
discarded. If the personnel department is substituted for the behaviour of
the inspector, it will eagerly avoid a *false alarm*. This would mean, in
terms of the intelligence test, that someone is accepted with an IQ that is
too low. The "solution" is that a high marginal score is agreed for the test
which involves many errors, but that is only annoying for the applicant and

not for the firm. With an eye to this, it is perhaps more reasonable to set
out a number of requirements which the applicants must meet, place on a list
those who are to be considered, and select the person in question randomly.

Equality

As is known, the nature theory says that intelligence is hereditarily
determined and is a necessity in obtaining diplomas. Educational
opportunities, income distribution, and differences between classes also
have to do with inheritance, and little can be done about this. Burt[6] states
that the chance of ending up in higher education is approximately five times
larger for the higher social classes, and he finds that excellent because
class differences are unavoidable in any civilized society. Husén points out
that there still is a reason for some further considerations because in the
OECD countries the chance in question would be as much as 25 times as large.
Also, in Russian society something similar can be see, although less
spectacular. According to Husén 20% of the pupils originate from the working
classes and that would partly come about because a criterion is employed for
admittance that has to do with a mysterious factor, namely the "produced
merits for the strengthening of the power of the people". Husén further
claims that the inequality in Russia during the last decades has increased.
Words and deeds are perhaps not the same.

In the United States a strange development has arisen concerning this[7].
When there was a desire to limit the immigration in the 20's in connection
with, among other things, the fear of the "swarm of Polish Jews" (Stoddard,
see chapter 1), hereditarian and eugenic thinking blossomed. Decreasing of
inequality between races and classes must not be strived towards because
everyone earned his genetic fate or God had wanted it that way, which also
led to the laissez-faire economy. After World War II, however, a large
shortage of employment for skilled labour developed, and on top of that the
Sputnik shock was added. One of the possibilities to do something about this
was that the negro received more opportunity in society. For that purpose it
was necessary that he was seen a priori as somewhat less inferior, to which
end the environmental theories were used[8]. In the Civil Rights Act of 1964
the United States Commissioner of Education was asked to find out which
factors have to do with the strongly unequal educational opportunities for
groups differing in race, skin colour, religion, and country of origin. One
of the results consisted of the gigantic compensation programs such as Head

Start.

Husén notes that "more equality" can be conceived of in at least three ways. The first is equality with arrival at school. This is not the case and it does not seem to be simple to strive for something like this. The least that is necessary for this (at least theoretically) holds that the upbringing's freedom of the parents is strongly impeded, and that a new generation of agogics, pedagogues, street-corner workers, and social workers rise to the level of pathetic TV people, who force all parents to treat their children uniformly with their incoherent jargon. A second type of equality has to do with educational opportunity and treatment at school, in which respect a number of possibilities in any case has not been studied. The third type of equality aims at results in terms of, for example, the income, because for the time being we can neither do without the garbage collector nor the physicist. Husén feels that in attempts to demolish thresholds, too much attention has been given everywhere to material facilities, while the psychological barriers would be much greater. More important than money and grants are, according to him, the aspirations of parents and children as well as the attitude of the teaching staff in relation to children from various social groups.

Others[9] say that the cry for equal chances carries the problem along with it that everyone seems to implicitly understand something different. Schematically, four possibilities could be distinguished.

		Goals	
		Equal for all	Individually different
Paths	Equal for all	A	B
	Individually different	C	D

A. This means elimination of most occupations and the denial of individual differences in aptitude and interest, and is therefore unrealistic.

B. In this case, the same educational time period for all can be conceived of but the goals become differentiated as an outcome of, again, aptitude and interest. Because of the long educational period many will become "overeducated" for many of the present occupations which is rather awkward unless a large number of occupations are abolished, which also carries many problems along with it.

C. Now the same goal must be strived for along various paths, for example, according to the learning possibilities and styles that a child

demonstrates. This does individual preferences an injustice and, moreover, it would (once more) be boring if everyone had the same occupation.
D. The variable goals and the variable paths appear to be connected to the
differences which do exist between people, for whatever reason. The so-
called pluriformity of society in the form of countless occupations is
maintained, but instead of *equal* opportunities everyone receives the
best opportunities, and that is not the same. Equal chances provide, so
far at least, no equal results. It can be stated in another way: one
receives an equal chance to take part in unequal education.

Talent Reserves

In an extension of this lies the difficult question about the talent
reserves possessed by a society. Husén feels that there is such a reserve
insofar that at elementary schools many children are encountered with a high
IQ who will later belong to the manual labourers. In England it would have
been found that of a group of 10,000 children 22% had an IQ of 135 and higher, but that only a small percentage ended up later in higher occupational
groups[10]. According to Husén, an important reason was that the teacher
often did not recommend sending children from lower social classes on to
higher education (*the* prejudice, thus), after which the parents followed
this advice. The problem is that there are low correlations between the IQ
of the child and the motivation and the aspiration of the parents.

Also in The Netherlands calculations or at least estimations have been
made of the intellectual reserve[11]. As a point of departure, 222,476 recruits
for the military service were used who, between 1947 and 1949, were tested
with the Raven, technical insight tests, mathematics, language, and
administrative tests. First, IQ appears to be unequally distributed over the
country. Regarding both tails of the distribution, a division of the country
into 78 economic-geographical areas brought a dispersion to light with a
factor 12. The lowest IQ was encountered in a fisherman's village (Urk),
which was not to be expected looking at the very high average incomes of
these fishermen. In general, a low intelligence was found in the rural
areas, within the small to very small (mixed) farms, and in closed com-
munities with few educational facilities. The larger and smaller (commuter)
cities scored the highest, whereby both schooling possibilities as well as
selective migration from rural areas can be thought of.

Research on 65,363 boys who passed the draft of 1952 showed that the

highest IQ was found with the independent occupations, teaching staff, and
the lowest with farmers and other agricultural workers. In general, it
applied that there was a very high correlation between the number of
possibilities to pursue a higher education in a region and the average IQ.
Further for example, sons of farmers who did not wish to practise the
occupation of their father, had a much higher intelligence than their
brothers who had remained in the same occupational class. Absolutely seen,
much intellect was present in the (amply manned) working class. According
to the authors, on the grounds of the norms employed at the time, as high as
30% were undereducated of those who, in regard to their IQ, belonged to the
highest 10% of the population, which appears therefore to mean a substantial
talent reserve. The same was the case with the following 20% of the distribution, and from the whole draft as much as 12% had received less
education than was possible with the IQ. Of the labourers sons, 2% followed
secondary education, while 8% could have easily managed this. The sons of
teaching staff had a sufficiently high IQ for those schools in 48% of the
cases, while 58% followed such education. The latter is interesting:
children from higher social levels are threatened with *overeducation* and
the lower strata with *undereducation*. It is strange that in different
calculations of the intellectual reserve, there is a correspondence with
Augustinus' doubts about whether a woman has a soul because the girls are
sometimes omitted, while this still always concerns approximately half of
the population.

Van Heek et al.[12] describe and analyse ten views of this streaming
issue in an extensive study. A few examples are the following: The biological
viewpoint holds that there are hardly any talent reserves and that consequently the underrepresentation of the lower social classes within high
school and college emerges from a too low, genetically determined intelligence. The authors do not agree with this proposition. Between 1942 and
1960 50% more children from this group go to high school and college which,
departing from a genetic explanation, appears improbable. Moreover, according to their judgment the limits have presumably not been reached yet. In
the United States and in Sweden relatively more labourers children stream
on to higher levels of education. This is attributed to the late division
of school types. In Switzerland the streaming-on figures in the last decades,
however, nothing has changed. This difference is also in conflict with the
hypothesis of an hereditary disposition.

The optimistic view says that the educational opportunities for all

groups are optimal at present. Van Heek et al. cannot endorse this either;
the chance of ending up in higher education is, according to them, 15 times
greater if one originates from the higher social milieus. The view of meritocracy based on IQ is rejected. Academics originating from lower milieus
manage well, they do not change their jobs excessively, and they are not
overrepresented in the lowest income brackets of their occupational group.
Their political preferences lie approximately between those of their parents
and academics who originate from higher social levels, which means that they
vote relatively "left-wing". Rigorous selection of children during lower
school age is highly discouraged. The test is not only unreliable in many
respects, but the (many) "late-flowering" drop out with this procedure.

As an explanation for the underrepresentation of the lower classes in
secondary education a number of points are indicated. Financial thresholds
cannot be seen (anymore) as an important inhibiter. Also according to them,
of much greater importance is the attitude of the parents. They do not
reject higher education as such, but they are very uncertain about the
capabilities of their children. This means that the decision is often
placed in the hands of the teacher or the child himself. Only a small
minority of these parents is further prepared to, and are capable of
exercising control over the homework, and there is little patience with set-
backs, which means that many children must leave high school if they fail
once. That the unknown is unpopular appears from the fact that (the few)
manual labourers with an extended education allow their children to stream
on much more easily. The same applies to parents who have acquaintances in
a higher milieu. Finally, as a general problem it is indicated that the
language usage and the vocabulary within lower social classes is often of
such a nature that the children already have problems in primary school.

Van Heek et al. do say, however, that the *very* eligible children from
all milieus receive sufficient opportunities to stream on to high school
and college. This pronouncement has been seriously challenged[13]. The
calculations of Van Heek are based on a prediction score consisting of
school performance, test results, the opinion of the teacher, and information about the milieu. A low social class is seen as a counter-indication,
which makes the analysis unfair. If only the *performance* of the children is
taken into consideration, there certainly does seem to be a large difference
between social classes. With the eligible sons of unskilled labourers 45.5%
stream on, but within the higher occupational groups the percentage is even
higher than can be maximally expected on the grounds of performance, and as

high as 134.2%. With girls these boundaries lie even further apart, namely
between almost 0 and 157.7%. Again, the phenomenon is encountered that
children from higher social classes run the risk of becoming overeducated.
Moreover, girls follow secondary education proportionately much less, which
is to be expected on the grounds of traditional role expectations[14]. However,
if the children are admitted there is hardly any variation in the chance of
obtaining a diploma as a function of social class. An unsolved problem is
that theoretical calculations are concerned here, in view of the fact that
the predictive validity of the (in this case) chosen measure for "performance" is not precisely known.

Ideology

The IQ debate has never been a scientific and "sober" conflict but for
an important part a battle between ideologies which in many respects are
incompatible. Therefore, there is no reason to doubt that the issue will
still drag on for long. In no single subject within psychology do facts and
norms seem to be so strongly interwoven, which will also be the reason that
almost every book about intelligence is biased in the one or the other
direction. Two ideologies stand opposite one another, and that has already
been the case for a century.

The conservative-liberal or elitist meritocracy holds that man is given
talents which can be measured and which are reflected by the social position.
Everyone receives approximately what he deserves by virtue of his fate. The
will to go higher soon becomes vanity; the talent reserve is limited,
expansion of education is a waste of money, selection is necessary to
identify and to educate the necessary problem-solvers and genius will emerge
anyway. The world is a genetic lottery. The egalitarian or, if you like,
socialistic concept aims more at the collective, divided responsibility, and
cooperation, and feels that environmental variables ought to take a central
position in educational policy. The great importance of the problem-solver
is not considered as such, nor the skewed income distribution which has to
do with that. In principle, talent can be made where shortage exists. Meritocracy is rejected, democratization and equality as goals, are central.
The world is a social lottery, for the time being.

From a content-psychological viewpoint, these views can hardly be judged because they are not related to facts but to desires. These are so
dominant that one can hardly speak of *data*. Various trends produce their own

facts, and the same figures are interpreted by different researchers in divergent ways resulting in, among other things, contradictory recommendations to the government. In the area of intelligence, values and facts are interwoven from the first phase of the study.

What now?

The key issue is what must be done and what in particular should be given attention in the future. The answer is (once more) not obvious and is (once more) an issue of the philosophy of science. If we attempt to overlook the history of psychology, the subject does appear in some respects to be a dangerous science. Apparently it is possible, on the grounds of inept presuppositions and research methods to influence the individual and society of which one, in any case partly, can only be ashamed. Moreover, the manner in which various historians have been successful in pretending that trends such as eugenics and social Darwinism have never existed, can be called nothing but perplexing.

The correlationist represents, for a century, a trend interested in the prediction of behaviour and individual differences. Instruments concerned with a low definition level are satisfactory in the framework of his point of view. The discussed material brings us to the conclusion that this approach, in view of the intelligence issue, has not been very satisfactory; diverse tasks of psychology have already taken another road long ago. The test will measure something but it is not known precisely what, and the descriptive and predictive value is low. There is hardly any intelligence theory and that is because it is incorrect to think that a theory will come about on its own if a million numbers are collected, a computer is used, and a package of statistical tests are purchased.

The cognitivist is an antipode insofar that he wishes to know *how* behaviour comes about, without immediately linking it with predictions (although the first can imply the second). Further, he is not concerned in the first instance with the individual, but with processes occurring in the species. If it is to be known what intelligence actually is, and what heredity and milieu *mean*, this approach is an alternative. It is perhaps of more interest to find out which processes have to do with the concepts which have been discussed so easily and for so long. For that purpose, it is about time to disregard the tests, factor analyses, and recommendations and go into the laboratory, instead of wildly coming up with more and more item styles. The first steps in this context have been taken (compare chapter 2), but the majority is still to come. It is much more interesting to understand differences than to suffice with the confirmation that they exist.

Footnotes, Chapter 9

1. Elshout (1976)
2. Brody and Brody (1976)
3. Bloom (1974)
4. De Klerk (1979)
5. Husén (1975)
6. Burt (1970)
7. Pastore (1949)
8. Blum (1978)
9. Klauer (1978)
10. Something must be wrong here because, looking at the IQ distribution, this is not possible.
11. See Idenburg and Zeegers (1951, 1957)
12. Van Heek et al. (1972)
13. Van Kemenade and Kropman (1972), Boon van Ostade (1972), Kropman and Collaris (1974), Collaris and Kropman (1978)
14. For a survey of rather drastic differences in this area see Warries (1979).

REFERENCES

Adams, B., Ghodson, M., Richardson, K.
1976 The evidence for a lower upper limit of heritability of mental test
performance in a national sample of twins.
In: Nature, 263, 5575, 314-316

Allen, G.E.
1975 Genetics, eugenics and class struggle.
In: Genetics, 79, June, 29-45

Anastasi, A.
1976 Common fallacies about heredity, environment, and human behavior.
In: A. Mehrens (ed.), Readings in measurement and evaluation in
education and psychology. (Holt, Rinehart and Winston, New York)

Anastasi, A., Foley, J.P.
1948 A proposed reorientation in the heredity-environment controversy.
In: Psychological Review, 55, 5, 239-249

Andriessen, E., Bleichrodt, N., Flier, H. van der,
1973 Intelligentie en intelligentieverschillen
In: Intermediair, 9

Baird, L.L.
1972 Review of the remote associates test.
In: Mental Measurement Yearbook, 445

Belmont, L., Marolla, F.A.
1973 Birth order, family size, and intelligence
In: Science, December, 96-1101

Bereiter, C.
1970 Genetics and educability: educational implications of the Jensen
debate.
In: J. Hellmuth (ed.), Disadvantaged child, vol. 3, (Bruner and Mazel,
New York)

Berg, J.H. van den
1964 Leven in meervoud
(Callenbach Nijkerk)
1970 Wat is psychotherapie?
(Callenbach Nijkerk)

Bernard, W., Leopold, J.
1962 Test yourself
(Chilton Company, New York)

Block, N.J.
1976 Fictionalism, functionalism and factor analysis

    In: R.S. Cohen et al. (eds.), PSA, 1974, 127-141 (Reidel, Dordrecht)

Bloom, B.S.
1974 Time and learning
    In: American Psychologist, 29, 682-688

Blum, J.M.
1978 Pseudoscience and mental ability
    (Monthly Review Press, New York)

Boon van Ostade, A.H.
1972 Het milieu en de overgang van het basis- naar het voortgezet onderwijs
    in Nederland
    In: Sociologische Gids, 19, 211-218

Bouterwek, H.
1943 Erbe und Persönlichkeit, charakterologische Ergebnisse der Zwillings-
    forschung
    (Deuticke, Wien)

Bowles, S., Gintis, H.
1972- IQ in the U.S. class structure
1973 In: Social Policy, November-February, 65-96

Broadhurst, P.L., Fulker, D.W., Wilcock, J.
1974 Behavior genetics
    In: Annual Review of Psychology, 389-415

Brody, E.B., Brody, N.
1976 Intelligence
    (Academic Press, New York)

Broman, S.H., Nichols, P.L., Kennedy, W.A.
1975 Presschool IQ, prenatal and early developmental correlates
    (Erlbaum, Hillsdale)

Burt, C.
1958 The inheritance of mental ability
    In: American Psychologist, 13, 1-15
1962 Francis Galton and his contributions to psychology
    In: The British Journal of Statistical Psychology, 15, 1-49
1970 Black paper two: the crisis in education
    In: C.B. Cox, A.E. Dyson (eds.) The Critical Quarterly Society, London
1971 Quantitative genetics in psychology
    In: The British Journal of Mathematical and Statistical Psychology,
    24, 1-21
1973 The structure of the mind. The evidence for the concept of intelligence
    In: S.Wiseman (ed.), Intelligence and ability (Harmondsworth, Penquin)

Burt, C. Howard, M.
1956 The multifactorial theory of inheritance and its application to
    intelligence
    In: The British Journal of Statistical Psychology, 8, 95-131
1957 The relative influence of heredity and environment on assessments of
    intelligence
    In: The British Journal of Statistical Psychology, 10, 2, 99-104

Buss, A.R.
1976 Galton and the birth of differential psychology and eugenics: social,
    political, and economic forces
    In: Journal of the History of the Behavioral Sciences, 12, 47-58

Campbell, D.T., Erlebacher, A.
1975 How regression artifacts in quasi-experimental evaluation can mistaken-
     ly make compensatory education more harmful
     In: E.L. Struening, M. Guttentag (eds.), Handbook of evaluation
     research, (Sage Publications, London)

Cattell, R.B.
1971 Abilities: their structure, growth, and action
     (Houghton, Mifflin, Boston)

Clarke, A.M., Clarke, A.D.B.
1976 Early experience
     (Open Books, London)

Cleary, T.A., Humphreys, E.G., Kendrick, S.A., Wesman, A.
1975 Educational uses of tests with disadvantages students
     In: American Psychologist, 30, 1, 15-41

Coleman, J.S.
1968 The mathematical study of change
     In: H.M. Blalock, A.B. Blalock (eds.), Methodology in social research
     (McGraw-Hill, New York)

Collaris, J.W.M., Kropman, J.A.
1978 Van jaar tot jaar
     (Intitute for Applied Sociology, Nijmegen)

Colman, A.M.
1972 Scientific racism and the evidence on race and intelligence
     In: Race, 14, 2, 137-153

Conway, J.
1958 The inheritance of intelligence and its social applications
     In: The British Journal of Statistical Psychology, 11, 2, 171-190

Cowan, R.S.
1972 Francis Galton's statistical ideas: the influence of eugenics
     In: Isis, 63, 509-528

Cronbach, L.J.
1970 Essentials of psychological testing
     (Harper & Row, New York)

Daniels, N.
1976 IQ, heritability and human nature
     In: R.S. Cohen et al. (eds.), PSA 1974, 143-180 (Reidel, Dordrecht)

Diesfeldt, H.F.A., Cahn, L.A., Cornelissen, A.J.E.
1978 Over onderzoek naar het effect van piracetam (Nootropil (R)) in de
     psychogeriatrie
     In: Nederlands Tijdschrift voor Gerontologie, 9, 2, 80-89

Donaldson, M.
1978 Children's minds
     (Fontana, Glasgow)

Dorfman, D.D.
1978 The Cyril Burt Question: new findings
     In: Science, 201, 4362, 1177-1186

Drenth, P.J.D.
1975 Inleiding in de testtheorie
     (Van Loghum Slaterus, Deventer)

1976 De psychologische test
     (Van Loghum Slaterus, Deventer)

Dumont, J.J.
1972 Leerstoornissen
     (Lemniscaat, Rotterdam)

Dumont, J.J., Hamers, J.H.M., Ruijssenaars, A.J.J.M.
1977 Rekenstoornissen
     In: Paedagogische Studiën, 54, 386-397

Duncan, O.D., Featherman, D.L., Duncan, B.
1972 Socioeconomic background and achievement
     (Seminar Press, New York)

Eaves, L.J.
1969 The genetic analysis of continuous variation: a comparison of experi-
     mental designs applicable to human data
     In: British Journal of Mathematical and Statistical Psygology, 22, 2,
     131-147

Eckland, B.K.
1967 Genetics and sociology: a reconsideration
     In: American Sociological Review, 32, 3, 173-194

Elshout, J.J.
1976 Karakteristieke moeilijkheden in het denken
     (Ph.D. thesis, University of Amsterdam)

Emigh, T.H.
1977 Partition of phenotypic variance under unknown dependent association
     of genotypes and environments
     In: Biometrics, 33, 505-514

Erlenmeyer-Kimling, R.L., Jarvik, L.F.
1963 Genetics and intelligence: a review
     In: Science, 142, 177-179

Eysenck, H.J.
1973 The inequality of man
     (Maurice Temple Smith, London)
1977 Intelligence, education and the genetic model
     (Unpublished manuscript, Leiden)
1978 Development and anticipation in psychology: the role of the psycholo-
     gist in society
     In: De Psycholoog, November, 531-547

Fisher, R.A.
1918 The correlations between relatives on the supposition of Medelian
     inheritance
     In: Transactions Roy. Soc. Edinburgh, 52, 399-433

Freeman, F.N., Holzinger, K.J., Mitchell, B.C.
1928 The influence of environment on the intelligence, school achievement
     and conduct of foster children
     In: Yearbook Nat. Soc. Study Educ., 27, 1, 103-217

Freudenthal, H.
1976 Intellektuele bekwaamheden niet bewijsbaar erfelijk
     (NRC Handelsblad, May 8)

Fruchter, B.
1954 Introduction to factor analysis   (Van Nostrand, Princeton)

Fulker, D.W.
1975 The science and politics of IQ
     In: American Journal of Psychology, 88, 505-537

Furby, L.
1973 Interpreting regression toward the mean in developmental research
     In: Developmental Psychology, 8, 2, 172-179
1973 Implications of within-group heritabilities for sources of between-
     group differences: IQ and racial differences
     In: Developmental Psychology, 9, 1, 28-37

Furth, H.G.
1973 Piaget, IQ and the nature-nurture controversy
     In: Human Development, 16, 61-73

Gagné, R.M.
1975 The conditions of learning
     (Holt, Rinehart and Winston, London)

Gaillard, A.W.K., Sanders, A.F.
1975 Some effects of ACTH 4-10 on performance during a serial reaction
     task
     In: Psychopharmacologia, 42, 201-208

Gaillard, A.W.K., Varey, C.A.
1977 Some effects of Org. 2766 on various performance tasks
     Report IZF, Soesterberg 18.

Galton, F.
1869 Hereditary genius. An inquiry into its laws and consequences
     (World, Cleveland)
1872 Statistical inquiries into the efficacy of prayer
     In: The Fortnightly Review, August 1, 125-135
1874 English men of science: their nature and nurture
     (Macmillan, London)
1883 Inquiries into human faculty and its development
     (Macmillan, London)
1889 Natural inheritance
     (Macmillan, London)

Gent, B. van
1978 Zonder kritiek vaart niemand wel
     (Universitaire Pers, Leiden)

Gray, J.
1974 In: Hoger Onderwijs Cahiers, 3, 13, 34-41

Groot, A.D. de
1970 Het eigen vooroordeel en de strijd daartegen
     In: Wijsgerig Perspectief, 11, 20-37
1972 De noodzaak van selectie. Selectie voor en in het hoger onderwijs
     (Staatsuitgeverij, 's-Gravenhage)

Groot, A.D. de, Peet, A.A.J. van
1974 De toekomst van de individuele verschillen
     (Amsterdam, R.I.T.P. Memorandum, 46)

Guilford, J.P.
1967 The nature of human intelligence
     (McGraw-Hill, New-York)

Halsey, A.H.
1958 Genetics, social structure and intelligence
    In: British Journal of Sociology, 9, 1, 15-28

Hays, W.L.
1977 Statistics
    (Holt, Rinehart and Winston, London)

Heek, F., et al.
1972 Het verborgen talent
    (Boom, Meppel)

Herrnstein, R.J.
1971 IQ
    In: Atlantic Monthly, September
1972 Comments on professor Layzer's Science or superstition
    In: Cognition, 1, 419-421
1973 IQ in the meritocracy
    (Little, Brown, Boston)

Hirsh, J.
1967 Behavior-genetic, or 'experimental' analysis: the challenge of
    science versus the lure of technology
    In: American Psychologist, 22, 2, 118-130

Hogarth, R.M.
1974 Monozygotic and dizygotic twins reared together: sensitivity of
    heritability estimates
    In: The British Journal of Mathematical and Statistical Psychology,
    27, 1-13

Holland, J.L.
1972 Review of the Torrance tests of creative thinking
    In: Mental Measurement Yearbook, 448

Holland, J.L., Nichols, R.C.
1964 Prediction of academic and extra-curricular achievement in college
    In: Journal of Educational Psychology, 1, 55-65

Honzik, M.P.
1957 Developmental studies of parent-child resemblance in intelligence
    In: Child Development, 28, 215-228

Hoorn, W. van, Meulman, J., Vincent, B.
1978 De maatschappelijke ontwikkeling van de psychologie
    (Psychological Institute, University of Leiden)

Hoorweg, J.C.
1976 Protein-energy malnutrition and intellectual abilities
    (Mouton, The Hague)

Hopkins, K.D.
1969 Regression and the matching fallacy in quasi-experimental research
    In: The Journal of Special Education, 3, 4, 329-336

Hoyt, D.P.
1965 The relationship between college grades and adult achievement. A
    review of the literature
    ACT Research Report, 7

Humphreys, L.G.
1978 To understand regression from parent to offspring, think statistically
    In: Psychological Bulletin, 85, 6, 1317-1322

Hunt, J.McV.
1961 Intelligence and experience
     (Ronald Press, New York)

Husén, T.
1975 Social influences on educational attainment
     (Organisation for Economic Co-operation and Development)

Idenburg, Ph.J., Zeegers, G.H.L.
1951, Begaafdheidsonderzoek en intelligentiespreiding
1957 (De Haan, Utrecht/Zeist)

Jaspars, J.M.F.
1975 Gelijkheid en ongelijkheid in de psychologie: het IQ-debat
     In: J. v.d. Doel, A. Hoogenwerf (red.), Gelijkheid en ongelijkheid
     in Nederland
     (Samson, Alphen a/d Rijn)
1976 Wordt intelligentie bepaald door erfelijkheid, opvoeding of fraude?
     In: NRC Handelsblad, November 20
1977 Onderwijs en de IQ controverse
     In: Weekblad voor leraren, September

Jencks, C.
1972 Inequality: a reassessment of the effect of family and schooling in
     America
     (Basic Books, New York)

Jensen, A.R.
1969 How much can we boost I.Q. and scholastic achievement?
     In: Harvard Educational Review, 39, 1-123
1971 A note on why genetic correlations are not squared
     In: Psychological Bulletin, 75, 223-224
1972 Genetics and education
     (Methuen, London)
1972 The IQ controversy: a reply to Layzer
     In: Cognition, 1, 427-452
1974 Kinship correlations reported by Sir Cyril Burt
     In: Behaviour Genetics, 4, 1-28
1978 The current status of the IQ controversy
     In: Australian Psychologist, 13, 1, 7-27

Jinks, J.L., Fulker, D.W.
1970 Comparison of the biometrical genetical, Mava and classical approaches
     to the analysis of human behavior
     In: Psychological Bulletin, 5, 311-349

Jones, H.E., Bayley, N.
1941 The Berkeley growth study
     In: Child Development, 12, 167-173

Jongkees, L.B.W., Vandenbroucke, J.
1975 Codex Medicus
     (Elsevier, Amsterdam)

Juel-Nielsen, N.
1965 Individual and environment. A psychiatric-psychological investigation
     on monozygotic twins reared apart
     In: Acta Psychiatrica et Neurologica Scandinavia, Monograph Supplement
     183

Kamin, L.J.

1974 The science and politics of IQ
     (Wiley, New York)
1978 Comment on Munsinger's review of adoption studies
     In: Psychological Bulletin, 85, 1, 194-201

Kaye, K.
1976 The IQ controversy and the philosophy of education
     In: R.S. Cohen et al. (eds.), PSA 1974, 181-188
     (Reidel, Dordrecht)

Kemenade, J.A., Kropman, J.A.
1972 Verborgen talenten? Kritische kanttekeningen bij een onjuiste inter-
     pretatie
     In: Sociologische Gids, 19, 219-228

Kempthorne, O.
1978 Logical, epistemological and statistical aspects of nature-nurture
     data interpretation
     In: Biometrics, 34, 1-23

King, W.L., Seegmiller, B.
1973 Performance of 14-22 months-old black, firstborn male infants on two
     tests of cognitive development: the Bayley scales and the Infant
     Psychological Development Scale
     In: Developmental Psychology, 8, 317-326

Klauer, K.J.
1978 Gelijke kansen in het onderwijs
     In: Paedagogische Studiën, 55, 450-457

Klerk, L.F.W. de
1979 Inleiding in de onderwijspsychologie
     (Van Loghum Slaterus, Meppel)

Koestler, A.
1971 The case of the midwife toad
     (Pan Books, London)

Kohnstamm, D., Lem, T. van der, Cornelisse, M., Kleerekoper, L., Colland, V.,
Doef, S. van der
1976 Had de proefkreche effekt?
     (Dekker & Van de Vegt, Nijmegen)

Kroonenberg, P.M.
1979 Van theorie naar model naar gegevens naar model naar theorie
     (Unpublished manuscript, Leiden)

Kropman, J.A., Collaris, J.W.M.
1974 Van jaar tot jaar
     (Institute for Applied Sociology, Nijmegen)

Layzer, D.
1972 Science or superstition?
     In: Cognition, 1, 265-299
1972 A rejoinder to professor Herrnstein's comments
     In: Cognition, 1, 423-426
1972 Jensen's reply: the sounds of silence
     In: Cognition, 1, 453-473

Leeuw, J. de
1977 Some simple path models for biometrical genetics
     Reasonable models for unreasonable data

Models of psychometrical genetics
A path model for birth order, sibling and family size effects
On a test proposed by Jinks and Fulker
(Unpublished manuscripts, Leiden)
1979 Galton's 'Law of ancestral inheritance'
(Unpublished manuscript, Leiden)

Lehrman, D.S.
1953 A critique of Konrad Lorenz's theory of instinctive behavior
In: The Quarterly Review of Biology, 28, 4, 337-363

Lewis, M.
1973 Infant intelligence tests; their use and misuse
In: Human Development, 16, 108-118

Lewontin, C.
1975 Genetic aspects of intelligence
In: Annual Review of Genetics, 387-405

Linn, R.L.
1974 Unsquared genetic correlations
In: Psychological Bulletin, 81, 3, 203-206

Linschoten, J.
1964 Idolen van de psycholoog
(Bijleveld, Utrecht)

Lippman, W.
1975 The reliability of intelligence tests
In: C. Karier (ed.), Shaping the American Educational State
(MacMillan, New York)

Loevinger, J.
1943 On the proportional contributions of differences in nature and in
nurture to differences in intelligence
In: Psychological Bulletin, 40, 10, 725-756

Luria, A.R., Yudovich, F. Ia.
1959 Speech and the development of mental processes in the child
(Staples Press, London)

Lytton, H.
1977 Do parents create, or respond to differences in twins?
In: Developmental Psychology, 13, 5, 456-459

Magnusson, D., Backeteman, G.
1977 Longitudinal stability or person characteristics:
intelligence and creativity. Reports of the Dept. of Psychology,
University of Stockholm, 511, December

McAskie, M., Clarke, A.M.
1976 Parent-offspring resemblances in intelligence: theories and evidence
In: British Journal of Psychology, 67, 2, 243-273

McCall, R.B., Robert, B., Appelbaum, M.I., Hogarth, P.S.
1973 Developmental changes in mental performance
In: Monographs of the Society for Research in Child Development, 38, 3,
150, 1-84

Medawar, P.B., Medawar, J.S.
1977 The life sciences
(Harper & Row, New York)

Meertens, C.J.
1977 Een onverstoorbare stoornis
(Institute for Developmental Psychology, Leiden)

Mendel, D.
1977 On measuring the unmeasurable
In: Higher Education Review, 1, 65-71

Milkman, R.
1978 A simple exposition of Jensen's error
In Journal of Educational Statistics, 3, 3, 203-208

Miller, J.K., Levine, D.
1973 Correlation between genetically matched groups versus reliability
theory
In: Psychological Bulletin, 79, 2, 142-144

Molenaar, I.W., Tomas, A.
1978 Psychometrics in subgroups, or regression to the mean revisited
In: Tijdschrift voor onderwijsresearch, 4, 152-160

Mönks, F.J., Knoers, A.M.P.
1978 Ontwikkelingspsychologie
(Dekker & Van de Vegt, Nijmegen)

Montagu, A.
1959 Human heredity
(The World Publishing Company, New York)
1975 (ed.) Race and IQ
(Oxford University Press, New York)

Munsinger, H.
1975 The adopted child's IQ: a critical review
In: Psychological Bulletin, 82, 5, 623-659
1977 The identical twin transfusion syndrome: a source of error in
estimating IQ resemblance in heritability
In: Annals of Human Genetics, 40, 307-321
1978 Reply to Kamin
In: Psychological Bulletin, 85, 1, 202-206

Nelissen, J.M.C.
1972 Aantekeningen bij compensatieprogramma's
In: Paedagogische Studiën, 49, 303-318
1977 Erfelijkheid en intelligentie
(Nieuwsbrief Psychologie en Maatschappij, december, 41-56)

Nelissen, J.M.C., Verloop, N., Zwarts, M.
1978 Intelligentie en rekenen: pleidooi voor een meer procesmatige benade-
ring van het intelligentiebegrip
In: Paedagogische Studiën, 55, 413-426

Newman, H.H., Freeman, F.N., Holzinger, K.J.
1937 Twins: a study of heredity and environment
(University of Chicago Press, Chicago)

Nienhuys, J.W.
1979 Some remarks on the confluence model of Zajonc and Markus
(Unpublished manuscript, Eindhoven)

Novitski, E.
1977 Human genetics
(MacMillan, New York)

Onians, R.B.
1951 The origins of European thought
     (Cambridge University Press, New York)

Overton, W.F.
1973 On the assumptive base of the nature-nurture controversy: additive
     versus interactive conceptions
     In: Human Development, 16, 74-89

Parreren, C.F., Bend, J.G. van der (eds.)
1978 Psychologie en mensbeeld
     (Basisboeken, Ambo, Baarn)

Pastore, N.
1949 The nature-nurture controversy
     (King's Crown Press, New York)
1978 The Army intelligence tests and Walter Lippmann
     In: Journal of the History of the Behavioral Sciences, 14, 316-327

Pearson, K.
1918 Inheritance of psychical characters
     In: Biometrika, 12, 367-372

Peet, A.A.J. van
1974 Het begrip intelligentie
     (Amsterdam, R.I.T.P. Memorandum 44)

Pinneau, S.R.
1961 Changes in intelligence quotient: infancy to maturity
     (Houghton Mifflin, Boston)

Posthumus Meyes, G.H.M.
1979 Quasi stellae fulgebunt
     (University Press, Leiden)

Putten, K. van, Rijnbeek, K.
1978 Klassikale tests en toetsen bij de overgang van het basisonderwijs
     naar het voortgezet onderwijs 1975-1976 in Nederland
     (Institute for Educational Psychology, Leiden)

Rao, D.C., Morton, N.E., Yee, S.
1974 Analysis family resemblances II. A linear model for family correlation
     In: American Journal of Human Genetics, 26, 331-359

Resnick, C.B. (ed.)
1976 The nature of intelligence
     (Erlbaum, New Jersey)

Riksen-Walraven, J.M.A.
1977 Stimulering van de vroeg-kinderlijke ontwikkeling
     (Swets en Zeitlinger, Amsterdam)

Ritter, H., Engel, W.,
1976 Genetik und Begabung
     In: H. Roth (ed.), Begabung und lernen. Band 4.
     (Ernst Klett Verlag, Stuttgart)

Rosenberg, C.E.
1976 No other Gods
     (Johns Hopkins University Press, Baltimore)

Rupp, J.C.C.
1969 Opvoeding tot schoolweerbaarheid

(Wolters-Noordhoff, Groningen)

Samelson, F.
1977 World War I intelligence testing and the development of psychology
     In: Journal of the History of the Behavioral Sciences, 13, 274-282

Sarason, S.B.
1976 The unfornate fate of Alfred Binet and school psychology
     In: Teachers College Record, 77, 4, 579-592

Scarr, S.
1968 Environmental bias in twin studies
     In: S.G. Vanderberg (ed.), Progress in human behavior genetics
     (Johns Hopkins University Press, Baltimore)

Scarr, S., Weinberg, R.A.
1976 IQ test performance of black children adopted by white families
     In: American Psychologist, 726-739

Scarr-Salapatek, S.
1971 Race, social class, and IQ
     In: Science, 174, 4016, 1285-1295

Schaie, K.W., Strother, C.R.
1968 A cross-sequential study of age changes in cognitive behavior
     In: Psychological Bulletin, 70, 671-680

Schmidt, W.H.O.
1973 Child development: the human, actual and educational context
     (Harper & Row, New York)

Schull, W.J., Neel, J.V.
1965 The effects of inbreeding on Japanese children
     (Harper & Row, New York)

Sherwood, J.J., Nataupsky, M.
1968 Predicting the conclusions of negro-white intelligence research from
     biographical characteristics of the investigators
     In: Journal Pers. Soc. Psychology, 8, 53-58

Shields, J.
1962 Monozygotic twins brought up apart and together
     (Oxford University Press, London)

Shockley, W.
1972 Dysgenics geneticity, raceology: a challenge to the intellectual res-
     ponsibility of educators
     In: Phi Delta Kappa, 53, 297-307

Skodak, M., Skeels, H.M.
1949 A final follow-up study of hundred adopted children
     In: Journal of Genetic Psychology, 75, 85-125

Smith, R.T.
1965 A comparison of socioenvironmental factors in monozygotic and dizygotic
     twins
     In: S.G. Vandenberg (ed.), Methods and goals in human behavior genetics
     (Academic Press, New York)

Snell, B.
1955 Die Entdeckung des Geistes
     (Claassen und Goverts, Hamburg)

Stanley, J.C.

1967 Problems in equating groups in mental retardation research
      In: The Journal of Special Education, 1, 241-256

Stein, Z., Susser, M.
1970 Mutability of intelligence and epidemiology of mild mental retardation
      In: Review of Educational Research, 40, 1, 29-67

Taylor, H.F.
1973 Playing the dozens with path analysis: methodological pitfalls in
      Jencks et al., Inequality
      In: Sociology of Education, 46, 433-450

· Tilborg, L.A.J. van
1977 Schattingen van genotypische intelligentie
      (Rotterdamse Mededelingen nr. 22, 1893)

Tversky, A., Kahneman, D.
1974 Judgment under uncertainty: heuristics and biases
      In: Science, 185, 1124-1131

Tyler, L.E.
1972 Human abilities
      In: Annual Review of Psychology, 23, 177-206

Ultee, W.C.
1977 Groei van kennis en stagnatie in de sociologie
      (Ph.D. thesis, University of Utrecht)

Urbach, P.
1974 Progress and degeneration in the IQ debate
      In: British Journal of Philosophical Science, 25, 99-135 and 235-259

Vandenberg, S.G.
1967 Hereditary factors in psychological variables in man, with a special
      emphasis on cognition
      In: J.S. Spuhler (ed.), Genetic diversity and human behavior
      (Aldine, Chicago)

Ven, H.H.G.S. van der
1976 Het meten van intelligentie door middel van tests met tijdslimiet
      In: Gedrag, 5-6, 260-277

Visser, R.A.
1978 Enkele opmerkingen bij het verschijnsel regressie naar het gemiddelde
      (Unpublished manuscript, Leiden)

Vroon, P.A.
1976 Bewustzijn, hersenen en gedrag
      (Basisboeken, Ambo, Bilthoven)
1978 Stemmen van vroeger
      (Ambo, Baarn)

Wade, N.
1976 IQ and heredity: suspicion of fraud beclouds classic experiment
      In: Science, 194, 916-919

Wagenaar, W.A.
1977 ACTH fragments and verbal learning
      (Report IZF, Soesterberg, 15)

Wagenaar, W.A., Timmers, H., Frowein, H.
1977 ACTH 4-10 and adaptive learning
      (Report IZF, Soesterberg, 13)

Wagenaar, W.A., Vroon, P.A., Janssen, W.H.
1978 Proeven op de som
     (Van Loghum Slaterus, Deventer)

Walberg, H.J., Marjoribanks, K.
1976 Family environment and cognitive development: twelve analytic models
     In: Review of Educational Research, 46, 4, 527-551

Warries, E.
1979 Studiekeuze en selectie: differentiële onderwijseffecten voor vrouwen
     en mannen
     In: Tijdschrift voor Onderwijsresearch, 4, 3, 97-112

Wied, D. de
1976 Hormonal influences on motivation, learning, and memory processes
     In: Hospital Practice, January, 123-131

Wilson, E.O.
1978 On human nature
     (Harvard University Press, Cambridge MA)

Winer, B.J.
1970 Statistical principles in experimental design
     (McGraw-Hill, London)

Wright, S.
1921 Systems of mating
     In: Genetics, 6, 111-178

Zajonc, R.B.
1976 Family configuration and intelligence
     In: Science, April, 227-236

Zajonc, R.B., Markus, G.B.
1975 Birth order and intellectual development
     In: Psychological Review, 82, 74-88